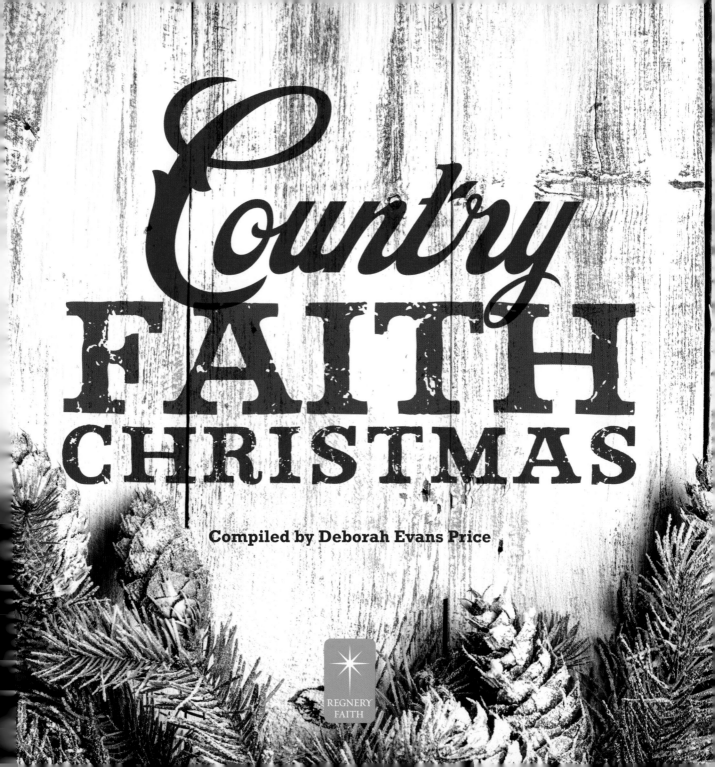

Country FAITH CHRISTMAS

Compiled by Deborah Evans Price

REGNERY FAITH

Regnery Faith™ is a trademark of Salem Communications Holding Corporation; Regnery® is a registered trademark of Salem Communications Holding Corporation

Scripture taken from the Holy Bible, NEW INTERNATIONAL VERSION®, NIV® Copyright © 1973, 1978, 1984, 2011 by Biblica, Inc.® Used by permission. All rights reserved worldwide.

Cataloging-in-Publication data on file with the Library of Congress

ISBN 978-1-62157-452-1

Published in the United States by
Regnery Faith
An imprint of Regnery Publishing
A Division of Salem Media Group
300 New Jersey Ave NW
Washington, DC 20001
www.Regnery.com

Manufactured in the United States of America

10 9 8 7 6 5 4 3 2 1

Books are available in quantity for promotional or premium use.
For information on discounts and terms,
please visit our website: www.Regnery.com.

Distributed to the trade by
Perseus Distribution
250 West 57th Street
New York, NY 10107

FOREWORD

I come from a family that loves and values our Christmas traditions. We have lots of them! The one which stands out the most from my childhood occurred on Christmas Eve at my grandmother's house. For about sixty years and without exception, my grandmother has hosted our ever-growing family in her house. My earliest memories are being a very excited little girl walking into her cozy country home. There I was met with hugs and Christmas greetings that, to this day, carry me from the front door all the way through the kitchen, where smells of turkey and dressing and every dessert imaginable fill the air. I learned if you are quick enough, you can sneak a pinch of a Christmas cookie or fried apple pie from the dessert table on your way in. The kitchen counters are covered with dishes—only to be rearranged as aunts, uncles, and cousins arrived with their "can't-do-without" family favorites.

These days there's a well-worn coffee table in grandmother's sunroom. That "kids table" welcomes additional scratches and spills which add to its character. There's a dining room table where my papa used to sit at the head with his permanent smile, greeting everyone who walked by. My grandmother, who's now ninety-two years old, takes her place with my daddy sitting on the opposite end. We know it's almost time to sit down to eat when Aunt Gail asks, "Who wants tea?" Of course, she unquestionably means sweet tea. But before we eat, we make a big circle around the table and join hands as Daddy says grace. He gives thanks for another year together, for the delicious goodness we are about to enjoy, and for the loving hands that prepared it.

When we sit down, the kids gobble up their food as fast as possible. They figure there's no sense wasting time eating when they could be opening up all those presents under the tree. I remember as a little girl impatiently begging, "Is it time to open presents yet?" I'd ask that question over and over all the while guessing at what might be under the tree for me. When the adults finally give in to the excitement of the children, we leave those "happy-face" plates, empty tea glasses, and crumbs behind and make our way into the living room where the gifts are given out—and the wrapping paper starts to fly in all directions.

These days, what's under the tree doesn't matter nearly as much to me as do the sweet faces that take up just about every inch of that beloved room. As my priorities have changed, I have learned to cherish these memories. Tears come to my eyes as the vivid pictures of Christmases past play in my mind. The love of God and family filling that old house is the greatest gift of all. And the Baby born in a lowly stable over two thousand years ago gives us every reason to keep that tradition going.

In the pages of *Country Faith Christmas*, my friends and fellow country artists join me in sharing their Christmas traditions, their beloved family photos, and their favorite Christmas recipes. So, find a quiet spot to sit back with a big glass of sweet tea or hot chocolate as we celebrate together the joy of Christmas through the greatest story ever told.

Kimberly Schlapman

DEDICATION

To my husband, Gary, and son, Trey, for their constant love and support. You fill my life with joy and keep the spirit of Christmas alive all year long. And to God, thanks for the gift of your precious son, Jesus—the reason for everything I do.

ACKNOWLEDGMENTS

My deepest thanks and love to all the artists and their families for the interviews, cherished photos, and personal recipes in this book. I appreciate everyone who so kindly shared their Christmas memories to make this project special.

Many thanks to my new friends at Regnery Faith—Bob DeMoss, Marji Ross, Mark Bloomfield, Maria Ruhl, Patricia Jackson, Emily Bruce, Jason Sunde, and John Caruso for the editing, publicity, production, cover design, and art direction of this beautiful book and for believing in this project; to Thom Schupp at CanOpener Creative for the interior design; to my Country Faith partners, Danny McGuffey, Adam Sicurella, and Joe Sicurella; to Janet Bozeman Media for the extra set of hands working the press opportunities; to Rod Riley and the team at WORD Entertainment; Ed Leonard and the gang at New Day Christian Distributors; to my transcriptionists Linda Partridge and Julie Price for typing all the interviews for the book; Laura Lung and Bob Siemon Designs for the wonderful jewelry; and my loving thanks to my parents Shirley and Bud Evans and

step-mom Garnett for cheering me across the finish line.

A heartfelt thanks goes to the managers and publicists without whom this book would have never happened: Alison Auerbach, Susan Bellamy, Darlene Bieber, Ailie Birchfield, Heather Bohn, Erin Burr, Allen Brown, Craig Campbell, Jaclyn Carter, Lori Christian, Amanda French Clark, Heather Conley, Katherine Cook, Vanessa Davis, Debbie Doebler, Craig Dunn, Kerri Edwards, Jami Fugate, Renee Behrman-Greiman, Don Murry Grubbs, Schatzi Hageman, Kathy Harris, Cindy Hart, Cindy Hunt, Kelly Russell Jarrell, Courtney Johanson, Mary Catherine Kinney, Les Martines, Jackie Marushka, Trisha McClanahan, Ebie McFarland, Martha Moore, Jackie Monaghan, Erin Morris, Jimmy Murphy, Dixie Owen, Jason Owen, Doug Paisley, Leigh Parr, Stephanie Rew, Jessie Schmidt, Scott Stem, Jensen Sussman, Paula Szeigis, Jennifer Vessio, Kyle Watson, Kirt Webster, Jeremy Westby, Celeste Winstead, and Nicole Zeller. If I forgot anybody, I'm sorry—and I'll buy you lunch!

CONTENTS

Photo: Russ Harrington

THE OAK RIDGE Boys

The Oak Ridge Boys were legends in gospel music long before they made the leap to country in 1977 with the hit "Y'all Come Back Saloon." Since then they've won numerous accolades including four ACM Awards, four CMA Awards, five Grammys, and nine Gospel Music Association Dove Awards. They were inducted into the Gospel Music Hall of Fame in 2000 and the Country Music Hall of Fame in 2015.

From left: Joe Bonsall, Duane Allen, William Lee Golden, and Richard Sterban.

William Lee GOLDEN (The Oak Rid

I come from a musical family. My grandparents and my parents all nurtured us with music. Granddaddy Golden was a fiddle player who played in barn dances as a young man. He even had a radio show with my sister and me. So music was always a part of our life growing up in Alabama. My mother's brothers played guitars and sang as far back as I remember.

I was about seven years old when we first got electricity—which was before we got running water. We had a battery-operated radio that we wouldn't run much during the week. But one of my earliest memories was listening on Saturday night to the Grand Ole Opry. My mother taught us to play instruments and by the time I was eight, I was playing guitar on the radio show with my granddaddy. We would sing gospel songs like "I Saw the Light."

At Christmas, we have always gathered together to sing and play music at the old home place. Even after my mother and dad passed away, two or three days after Christmas we still get together there in Alabama with my cousins. Everybody brings their instruments and food, and we all have a big time. The music starts early and lasts 'til late. It always was uplifting and it's the part of the holiday that we actually plan and look forward to. Another tradition is having one of the kids or grandkids read the Christmas story to everybody before opening any presents.

Above: William Lee Golden enjoys the season.
Right: As a boy in Alabama.

Joe BONSALL

(The Oak Ridge Boys)

As far as Christmas family traditions go, I don't think our family does anything special in comparison with everyone else. We enjoy dinner, the tree, decorations, presents, fun, family time, worship, and memories. It's my favorite time of the year for certain—a blessed time. I am very thankful for each year that God allows me to live to see another Christmas. As far as the Christmas story goes, I have always had a keen interest in God's holy angels. Ever since reading a book by Billy Graham many years ago, which was a study on these principalities of love and light, I have loved angels.

In my book of short stories, *Christmas Miracles*, an angel actually appears in four out of the six stories. If I had to picture a character from the Christmas story with whom I identify, it would have to be the shepherds tending their flocks when suddenly the sky filled with the heavenly hosts announcing the birth of Christ. My mind cannot even comprehend what that must have looked like

Above: Joe with his wife Mary. Left: Joe (holding puppy) enjoys Christmas with his family in Pennsylvania.

Photos: Courtesy Joe Bonsall

to these men. Try to envision a sky FULL of ANGELS, singing and praising God in the highest. So make me a shepherd, if you will, sitting beneath a tree on a dark night enjoying the soft sounds of insects and such when BOOM. Yes, I would love to have been there for that one. I can only imagine how fast I would have headed for that manger behind the inn.

Duane ALLEN

(The Oak Ridge Boys)

The Allen family Christmas for us is in Hendersonville, Tennessee, where my son and daughter live. They bring the grandkids over and my house turns into a zoo. Everybody has the run of the house. We always eat the Christmas meal together, pray together, and then we gather in the den. Before we all go into the den, Norah Lee finds the secret places where Santa Claus has hidden all the presents all year. Norah Lee and I help Santa Claus put the gifts in each of the chairs scattered around the den for all the kids and everybody else.

One of the greatest Christmases I ever had was the first house I lived in when we got married, back when we had our first child, Jamie. Our little girl was born on December 13. When Christmas morning came around that year, Norah Lee slipped out without waking me up. She went into the baby's room and dressed Jamie up real pretty for Christmas. She put her in a little bitty rocker and put her under the Christmas tree. Then, she came and woke me up, took me in there, and said, "Merry Christmas!" There was Jamie under the Christmas tree. That had to be the sweetest Christmas I've ever had and it's a good example of how we celebrate Christmas around here. It's all about family, it's all about love, it's all about God, and it's all about giving, sharing, and the story of Jesus Christ.

DONNA'S SEAFOOD SAUCE

The Oak Ridge Boys' Richard Sterban's Recipe

My mother was born in Italy. I was raised eating Italian food. There's an Italian tradition that on Christmas Eve you eat seafood. They call it the "Seven Fishes." Even my mother, who recently passed away, said that Donna's sauce was better than her own.

INGREDIENTS
Extra virgin olive oil
2–3 tablespoons minced garlic
2 boxes Pom's tomato puree
1 large can Pom diced tomatoes
2 tablespoons Herbs de Provence
2 tablespoons oregano
Salt and pepper, to taste
24 fresh mussels, washed, and with shells scrubbed
24 Cherry Stone or Little Neck Clams
24 shrimp, peeled and deveined

DIRECTIONS
Cover the bottom of a large pot with olive oil; add garlic. Lightly brown garlic. Add tomatoes and seasonings. Simmer for 30 minutes. Add shrimp, clams, and mussels. Cook until shrimp is pink and clams and mussels are open.
DO NOT EAT UNOPENED CLAMS OR MUSSELS.
Serve over freshly cooked pasta—with crusty Italian bread.
*To make Fra Diablo version, add 2–3 tablespoons of crushed red pepper.

Above left: Duane as a "young" cowboy.
Above: Richard Sterban with wife Donna.

Photos: Courtesy Richard Sterban

Photo: Jim Wright

CANAAN *Smith*

A native of Williamsburg, Virginia, Canaan Smith released his debut album, *Bronco*, in 2015 and scored his first No. 1 hit with the single "Love You Like That." A compelling songwriter, Smith's title track on *Bronco* was about his sixteen-year-old brother who died in a car accident when Canaan was eleven. He's written for Cole Swindell, Florida Georgia Line, and Jason Aldean and toured extensively with Darius Rucker, Dierks Bentley, and Florida Georgia Line.

I have such a big family. There were six kids and we were all around the same age, only a ten-year spread total between us. I was the fourth born. My mom had four kids under the age of five—and they were all boys—and then she had a girl fifth. She thought she was done but then she had a "surprise" boy later. Like other kids, we just felt it was magical at Christmas time. My mom would make chili on Christmas Eve—that big pot of chili was one of our traditions.

Since my folks always let us open one present the night before Christmas morning, we did everything from shaking the packages, weighing the packages—anything to just try to guess what was inside. I hate surprises. I love them, but I hate them, too. As much as I couldn't wait to open the presents, as much as I didn't want to know, I also couldn't stand waiting. So it was cool they let us open one on Christmas Eve.

My most memorable gift was a motorcycle as a kid and it changed my life. In fact, I got a motorcycle and a go-cart in the same year. We immediately made a dirt track in our backyard and just went around, around, and around. I lived for that. As soon as I got home from school that's all I did. It was just so much fun that we boys looked forward to.

My parents have always been super generous and

Photo: Courtesy Jim Wright

I just have been blessed to get to have Christmas in the first place, let alone with a loving family and presents under the tree. It's a lot to be grateful for. The older I get the more I realize how special it is and how important it is to take time to reflect on our blessings. A lot of families don't get to celebrate it like that. It was cool. I can't wait to do that with my family someday.

While I'm not a dad, for some reason Joseph is the character I most relate to in the Christmas story. I don't have a kid yet, but I can relate to Joseph because as a man he was doing everything in his power to get his wife a safe place to lie, a place to rest. They had traveled so far and the best he could do was practically a sheep pen. I identify with that as a man—with him wanting the best for the love of his life, and at the same time running up against the wall. There's something in that exhaustion that speaks to me.

CANAAN'S MOM'S CHRISTMAS CHILI

From my mom Cheryl Wilds

INGREDIENTS
2 pounds ground chuck
1 large yellow onion
2 tablespoons minced garlic
2 teaspoons cumin
1 teaspoon cinnamon
4 tablespoons chili powder
2 tablespoons Worcester sauce
2 15-ounce cans of kidney beans
2 28-ounce cans tomato sauce
2 28-ounce cans crushed tomatoes
Salt and pepper to taste

DIRECTIONS
In a large stock pot, brown the ground chuck, add chopped onion, minced garlic, Worcester sauce, and other spices. Add drained kidney beans, cover, and simmer for an hour and a half to two hours on low. Cook macaroni al dente and drain. Serve chili with macaroni, shredded cheese, salt and pepper, and chili powder to taste.

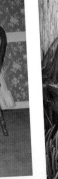

Photo: Courtesy Canaan Smith

Left to right: Andrew, Leah, Judah, Ben (youngest), and Canaan.

"*Joseph*
SON OF DAVID,
DO NOT BE AFRAID
TO TAKE *Mary* HOME AS YOUR WIFE,
BECAUSE WHAT IS CONCEIVED IN HER IS
from the Holy Spirit.
SHE WILL GIVE BIRTH TO A SON, AND YOU ARE TO GIVE
HIM THE NAME *Jesus,* BECAUSE HE WILL SAVE HIS
PEOPLE FROM THEIR SINS."

Matthew 1:20

Sara Evans

Sara Evans has sold more than six million albums and scored five No. 1 hits including "Suds In the Bucket," "A Real Fine Place to Start," and "A Little Bit Stronger," which spent two weeks at the summit and was certified Platinum. She's won numerous honors including the Academy of Country Music's Top Female Vocalist, the Country Music Association's Video of the Year for her chart-topping single, "Born to Fly," and she's been named one of *People* magazine's "50 Most Beautiful People."

Sara with kids: Avery, Olivia, Audrey.

Growing up in Missouri, our tradition was to go see my mom's parents every Christmas Eve. Granny and Pawpaw lived in Columbia, which was a forty-five-minute drive for us. Granny would cook the most amazing dinner! We'd get together with my mom's two brothers and my cousins and have this huge time opening gifts down in their big finished basement. That was the best night of the year. We did that growing up well into my adulthood. It was always such a special time. My granny passed away about four years ago and our traditions have changed.

Since Jay and I got married, we go to church on Christmas Eve and then out to dinner at this restaurant in Birmingham called Fleming's, so we make Christmas Eve kind of this fancy, get-really-dressed-up traditional kind of deal. A lot of times we'll open gifts with his mom and his sister and the cousins after Christmas Eve dinner. On Christmas morning, when I was growing up, my mom always made an enormous breakfast with everything you could possibly imagine—bacon, eggs, sausage, sausage gravy, biscuits,

I JUST LOVE ALL ASPECTS OF CHRISTMAS— NOT ONLY CELEBRATING THE BIRTH OF CHRIST, but the fun stuff that goes on WITH YOUR CHILDREN.

homemade cinnamon rolls, orange juice. Now I'm carrying on that Christmas morning tradition.

Christmas time has always been so special to me because we are celebrating the birth of Jesus. Without Him we are a lost world. I just love all aspects of Christmas—not only celebrating the birth of Christ, but the fun stuff that goes on with your children, especially when they are little. There's something that's so nostalgic about it, but we really, really have to remember that it started with Jesus coming to be a man and to be on Earth with us and that God sent Him. All of that is just so overwhelming. It's easy to forget that's what Christmas is all about which is why I love all of the religious Christmas songs—they're so powerful and they help us to never lose sight of what Christmas is really about. "O Holy Night" is my favorite.

When it comes to special Christmas gifts over the years, my main memory as a child is the time I got the Easy Bake Oven. That stands out in my

mind because we did not have money and I know that was a big deal for my mom to get me that gift. I remember thinking, "This is the best thing that has ever happened to me." Moms really do make a lot of sacrifices. No wonder I tend to identify with Mary in the Christmas story. As a mom, I know what she was going through and the stress of having to give birth and having nowhere to be and to take care of your baby. I've always thought, "My gosh! What an amazingly strong woman she must have been and how scary giving birth in a manger probably was for her."

Sara EVANS

REFRIGERATOR ROLLS

INGREDIENTS
1 package yeast
½ cup warm water
1 cup hot milk
½ cup sugar
1 cup light brown sugar
1 teaspoon cinnamon
½ teaspoon salt
2 eggs
5 cups flour
5 teaspoons melted shortening

DIRECTIONS
Dissolve sugar in hot milk, add two cups flour and stir well. Add eggs and beat well. Then add shortening and yeast that was dissolved in water, salt, and three more cups of flour. Mix and let rise to double. Put in fridge to use the next day.

Use this dough and roll out to large rectangle spread with stick of soft butter. Mix brown sugar and white. Add 1 heaping teaspoon of cinnamon. Sprinkle sugar mixture over butter. Roll dough up along long end of rectangle. Pinch dough together at seam when finished rolling. Cut off 1 to 2 inch strips on end of roll. Place in buttered baking dish. Let rise to double and bake at 350° F for about 20–25 minutes. Ice with powdered sugar icing by making icing thin enough to drizzle over rolls.

This will be a sign to you: **YOU WILL FIND A BABY, WRAPPED IN CLOTHS AND LYING IN A** *Manger.*

Luke 2:12

Photo: Jim Wright

Vince GILL

A member of the Country Music Hall of Fame, Vince Gill is a noted humanitarian, avid golfer, and prolific singer/songwriter who has sold more than 26 million albums and scored such hits as "When I Call Your Name," "I Still Believe in You," and "Go Rest High on that Mountain." Gill has won countless accolades, including eighteen CMA Awards and twenty Grammys—more than any other male country artist.

Growing up in Oklahoma, Christmas time was pretty normal. One thing I have never been able to forget is the sneakiness of my sister. She would always sneak down to the tree and open up all of the presents. She'd even open the tape and then re-tape everything—that way she knew everything she was getting. I knew she was doing it. I don't think Mom and Dad ever did.

I've got pictures of me at probably three or four years old getting my first football. My big brother was such a great big brother. He'd play football with me and love on me and those pictures cement the wonderful memories. I was nine or ten years old when I got the biggest Christmas gift ever—my own guitar. I can still remember the case when I opened it up for the first time and the Fender amp. That's just more precious than anything I've ever gotten for Christmas.

I played hard and practiced a lot. My parents really saw all of my interest in playing. What made it special was the fact that it was my guitar—not my dad's guitar that I was borrowing. It was mine—a Gibson ES 335—and I can remember every scratch I had ever put on it. These days it's down at the Country Music Hall of Fame and Museum. I still play that kind of guitar and model to this day. So to have gotten such a great tool of the trade at that young of an age was really something. I had no idea then how important that gift would become in my life and career.

These days, more than anything, the chance to see

slows down and comes over for a little while. Most of the time they spend the night before Christmas. We'll gather in the hallway for a kid picture every year. Amy does it all up right. I'm a novice. I just follow her. And, for fifteen years since Amy and I got married, we've had a Christmas tradition of me fixing a giant breakfast for everybody with hundreds of eggs, pounds and pounds of bacon, and rolls and everything. In 2014, I wasn't paying attention, I was opening some bacon and I cut the end of my thumb off.

It was pretty scary. My whole guitar life flashed before my eyes. And it was a little bit freaky for everybody, too. After I got all bandaged up and put back together, the kids all said, "You are officially fired." No longer is my being the breakfast chef our tradition. In spite of the occasional mishap, Christmas is my favorite time of the year. Everybody stops. It's the one holiday where everybody really does stop and takes stock of who their family is and what that means. It's the time of year when people stop and say, "Okay,

AMY'S BAKED GARLIC CHEESE GRITS

These will keep me around forever.

INGREDIENTS
4 eggs, beaten
½ cup milk
16 ounces Velveeta cheese, cubed
¼ teaspoon garlic powder
2 cups regular grits
¼ teaspoon pepper
1 teaspoon salt
6 cups chicken broth
1 stick butter
8 ounces grated sharp white cheddar cheese

DIRECTIONS
Preheat oven to 350° F.
Grease a 4-quart casserole dish. Bring broth, garlic powder, salt, and pepper to a boil in a 2-quart saucepan. Stir in the grits and whisk until completely combined. Reduce the heat to low and simmer until the grits are thick, about 8 minutes. Add the cubed Velveeta cheese and milk and stir. Gradually stir in the eggs and butter, stirring until all are combined. Pour the mixture into the prepared casserole dish. Sprinkle with the white cheddar cheese and bake for 35–40 minutes or until set.

Photo: Kristen Barlowe

THE WORD

became flesh and made

his dwelling among us.

WE HAVE SEEN HIS GLORY, THE GLORY OF

THE ONE AND ONLY SON,

who came from the

Father,

FULL OF GRACE AND TRUTH.

John 1:14

Photo: Courtesy Jimmy Wayne

Jimmy Wayne overcame a turbulent childhood and homelessness during his teen years to become a chart-topping country singer/songwriter well known for such hits as "I Love You This Much," and the No. 1 "Do You Believe Me Now." This North Carolina native is a passionate humanitarian and tireless advocate for children in the foster care system. In 2010, he launched the "Meet Me Halfway" campaign, walking over 1,700 miles from Nashville to Phoenix to raise awareness for foster kids and homeless youth. His book, *Walk To Beautiful* is a *New York Times* Bestseller.

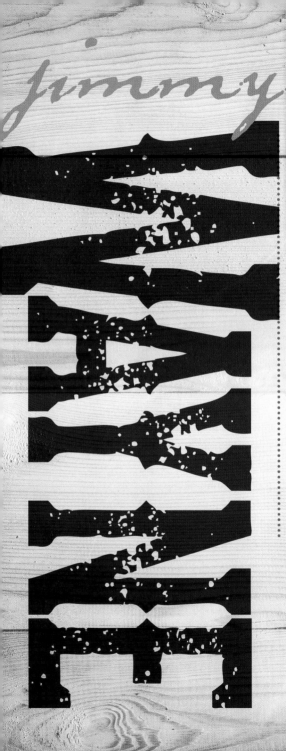

jimmy WAYNE

Unfortunately I don't have a lot of good Christmas memories growing up. I remember a lot of bad Christmases. We didn't get anything. Mom didn't even put up lights. I'd see the kids in the neighborhood with new bikes and new clothes and stuff. I remember going up the street looking at people's trash because I wanted to see the boxes of what those kids got. I'd just stare at the boxes thinking about the toy and wishing it was mine.

I did get things from the Salvation Army's "Angel Tree" program. It was great to be getting those bags of groceries and a few gifts. The Salvation Army provided me with my first guitar in 1987 when my sister and I were recipients of the "Angel Tree" program. Years later, I wrote a song called, "Paper Angels" because I wanted to raise awareness of that campaign which has been around since 1979.

The "Angel Tree" program is so important because if we don't help impoverished kids, they won't get anything for Christmas. When you see a person who is hungry, it doesn't matter who they are, where they come from, what color, boy or girl—you better do something to feed them. If you've got it and you don't give it, you'll answer for it.

When I was a seventeen-year-old homeless teenager, Bea and Russell Costner took me into their home, gave me a place to live, and helped me finish school. One gift that really stands out is a tool set that I received from Bea's daughter and son-in-law, Sandie and James Conrad. It's a Sears Craftsman tool set. I still have it, and it's now twenty-something years old. With that tool set I've worked on a lot of cars. I've changed engines and transmission out. I've changed spark plugs. I worked on the car that I drove to Nashville. I had an old Ford truck and I did a tune up with that tool set.

My most memorable Christmas was spent in prison—working as a guard, that is. I was single, living in North Carolina. The schedule gave me Christmas Eve and Christmas Day off. I didn't care about getting those days off since I didn't have a family. But a grandfather named Officer Robert Deal, who loved his kids and his grandkids, was going to have to work. I called him and said, "Let's trade days. I'll work Christmas Eve and Christmas for you.

> MY MOST MEMORABLE **CHRISTMAS** WAS SPENT IN **PRISON—** WORKING AS A GUARD, THAT IS.

Somewhere down the road if I need to make a trip to Nashville, I want you to work those two days for me." He agreed.

I showed up Christmas Eve for the shift briefing conducted by a cigar-smoking sergeant. He said, "Alright Jimmy, you've got A, B, and C dorms tonight." Walking the hallways that night was eerie. It was about 10:30 p.m. and the TVs weren't on. There wasn't a convict up playing poker or chess or board games. They weren't mingling—nothing. They were all in their cells, in their beds, covered up.

I thought that was so bizarre. I'd never seen this on a weekend night. Usually it's hustling, wheeling and dealing, slamming poker cards, and they're running all over the place. The silence was completely different, like the quiet before a storm. I thought it was spooky and I got a seriously dangerous feeling. I also noticed all the floors were especially clean and shiny with a reflection that you could comb your hair in.

I said to the sergeant, "Man, this place is different, ain't it?"

"This is what it's like here on Christmas Eve," he said. "They miss their families so

Photo: Courtesy Jimmy Wayne

much that they invest their energy in cleaning the floors—they went overboard because they had to stay busy. You stay busy or you'll go crazy and kill somebody."

At midnight the lights snapped off. Those things hum all night like white noise but other than that it was quiet. As I walked down the corridor, my big key ring was making the most noise. At the end of the corridor, I heard someone quietly starting to sing "Silent Night." I stopped as that melody echoed out from the cell of "Jelly Roll"—that was his nickname. He was a big black guy with one eye that was messed up, while the other one stared at you. He and his family were gospel singers.

As Jelly Roll continued to sing with a baritone voice like an old blues singer, I saw guys in there—felons who committed cold blood murders—lay in their beds and cry. When he hit that "all is calm" it rumbled throughout that entire prison. There wasn't a person making a sound. Men were listening and crying. He sang: "Sleep in heavenly peace, sleep in heavenly peace." I thought, "Man, that's the best Christmas

I've ever experienced in my life!"

By giving Officer Deal that night off he was blessed, and so was I. It's the gift of giving when you give somebody something and don't expect something in return. That was so amazing—the night Jelly Roll broke the silence of that silent night. As far as the Christmas story goes, I identify most with Jesus because that's who we are supposed to identify with the most. He was born homeless. He died homeless. He was a leader. He fought for what was right. He wasn't a coward and He loved everybody—whether or not they're behind bars at Christmas.

FAVORITE CHRISTMAS RECIPE

CAN OF CRANBERRY SAUCE

DIRECTIONS
Open can.
Serve.

BELLAMY *Brothers*

For more than four decades, Howard and David Bellamy have populated the radio with such memorable hits as "Let Your Love Flow," "I Need More of You," and "You Ain't Just Whistlin' Dixie." The Bellamys have more than fifty albums—including two gospel collections—and scored twenty No. 1 hits.

David

We had a pretty traditional Christmas, except for the fact that in Florida it was much warmer weather—so many years were spent having Christmas in the barn. That's a tradition we still carry on today—each year we have our Christmas dinner in Howard's barn. It's the closest thing to the manger. Church was always a really big part of our Christmas, we were in many Nativity scenes playing shepherds or wise men—and sometimes using our live farm animals in the stable.

Howard

We loved getting animals for Christmas. We got a horse once for Christmas. Being raised in the country, I think we liked getting animals the most: baby calves or chickens—and rabbits at Easter time. We always had lots of animals. Which might be why we identify with the shepherds, because they're the most like farmers.

David

We had a lot of traditions in our family growing up. We used to go caroling, of course, and we were always taking part in Christmas plays. We loved going to the woods to gather mistletoe and holly and we always harvested our own Christmas tree. It was always a time of year when our whole family—Howard and I, along with our dad and sister—would work up what they used to call a "special" and sing it at church. All of these things, along with the food our mom and dad cooked and the story of Jesus's birth, made Christmas really special and something we'll always remember.

But there was one other very special tradition we had that made it truly Christmas. One of the neighboring ranches had a couple of elderly men, Les and John, living in little shacks on their land. They'd help out the farmers and ranchers doing odd jobs. They were so poor they depended on help from poor farmers like us. Every Christmas morning my parents would get up really early and start cooking up turkey, dressing, sweet potatoes, and wonderful desserts. We'd all load up in the truck around 11a.m. and take food to these two old guys.

They were always so happy to receive the feast. Afterward we'd come back home and eat our dinner. We did it every Christmas. It was as much a part of our tradition as exchanging gifts. Bringing them that meal never seemed strange at the time but as the years went by and the two old men and our dad passed away, it took on even more meaning for us. Caring for Les and John has become one of our favorite memories of Christmas.

David Bellamy plays Santa Claus.
Photo: Courtesy David Bellamy

OYSTER DRESSING

INGREDIENTS
1 cup plain yellow cornmeal
1 cup all purpose flour
3 tablespoons sugar
1 tablespoon baking powder
½ cup unsalted butter
1 cup whole buttermilk

DRESSING INGREDIENTS
1 14-ounce bag herb
 season stuffing
1 cup unsalted butter
2 cups finely chopped
 sweet onion
1 ½ cups finely chopped celery
5 cups chicken broth
5 large eggs, lightly beaten
2 teaspoons dried sage
1 ½ cups chopped oysters
Salt and pepper

DIRECTIONS
Start by baking the buttermilk cornbread. Grease a 10" cast iron skillet and place it on the center rack of oven to 425°F. Then, in large mixing bowl combine the cornmeal, flour, sugar, baking powder, and salt. In a separate bowl, beat the eggs, melted butter, and buttermilk. Add the wet ingredients to the dry ingredients and stir until just incorporated. Pour the batter into the preheated skillet and smooth the top. Bake until cornbread is golden yellow, about 16 to 19 minutes. Don't overcook or dry out. Immediately remove the cornbread from skillet and allow to cool.

For cornbread oyster dressing, preheat oven to 350°F. Crumble the cornbread into small pieces (makes about 5 cups) and combine the crumbled cornbread and stuffing mix in an extra large bowl; toss to combine. Melt half of the butter in large skillet over medium heat. Add onion and celery and sauté, stirring frequently, until soft and translucent, about 10–12 min. Add the onion and celery to the cornbread mixture. Melt the remaining butter. In a large mixing bowl, combine the butter, chicken broth, eggs, sage, and oysters; whisk to combine. Add to the cornbread mixture and mix until thoroughly incorporated. Season generously with kosher salt and pepper. Pour into a greased 9 x 13 inch casserole dish. Bake uncovered, until the dressing is set and golden brown. About 45–50 minutes.

Glory
TO GOD IN THE
HIGHEST HEAVEN,
AND ON EARTH PEACE
to those on whom
HIS FAVOR
RESTS.

Luke 2:14

Photo: Courtesy Russ Harrington

The "Queen of Country" has sold more than 56 million albums worldwide and placed thirty-five singles at the top of the charts. Her 2015 album, *Love Somebody*, became her twelfth No. 1 on Billboard's Top Country Albums chart. In addition to being one of country music's most awarded female vocalists, she has found success in film, TV, and Broadway.

If I didn't have my relationship with the Lord, I don't know how I would function. He's my rock. He's my strength. He's my best friend. He's the one I talk to about every situation in my life, and I feel really confident and a lot stronger with that. He's the greatest thing in the world. I just don't know what I'd do without that relationship—which is why I'm so thankful for Christmas.

Our family likes to watch Christmas movies on Christmas Eve. Before we open gifts on Christmas morning, when all the kids get in there by the tree, we sing "Happy Birthday" to Jesus. My mother-in-law, Gloria Blackstock, bakes a cake for Jesus and we sing "Happy Birthday" to Jesus, which I think is a great thing to do. It's Gloria's tradition that she taught me.

I realize all of the kids are so anxious to be opening the gifts, ripping open the presents and all. But I just think it's a good time to make them stop, sit down, take a breath, and realize why we're celebrating Christmas. The meaning of Christmas isn't for you to get a lot of toys and a lot of stuff you really don't need. Which is why it's really good to sing Happy Birthday to Jesus—it's His birthday and that's where the cake idea comes in.

Of course with Christmas there are presents and

BEFORE WE OPEN GIFTS ON CHRISTMAS MORNING, WHEN ALL THE KIDS GET IN THERE BY THE TREE, WE SING *"Happy Birthday to Jesus."*

Santa, too. I have a little story I like to tell the kids. I've always said a little thing about how "Santy Claus" and Jesus get together and because Jesus gets so many gifts on His birthday, He shares them with the good little girls and boys all the way around the world. Santa Claus is the one who delivers the gifts.

Speaking of gifts, when we were younger—this was back in the '80s, my little sister Susie gave me my basketball shoes that I used when I played in twelfth grade in high school. I lived, slept, and breathed basketball. I don't know why she had them, but she had my old basketball shoes. I just sat there and cried. I thought it was so special of her to do that. We're both pack rats like our mama was—not as bad, but we are both pack rats. I guess she just cleaned out a closet or something and said, "I'm going to give these to Reba." The other thing I love are the cards that my son Shelby gives me. When he gives me a gift, he always writes me a card and puts it on top of it. I treasure those too.

Helping others, especially at Christmastime, is important to us. We give a lot to others anonymously. When a family is having a rough time, especially during Christmas, we like to help them out so that their kids can have gifts and things like that. Helping others is probably the greatest gift we can ever give.

FAVORITE CHRISTMAS RECIPE

Pigs in a Blanket

Last Christmas we started a new tradition. On Christmas morning when everybody gets there, they're hungry because they've been opening gifts at their house. So when they got to our house, the kids and I went into the kitchen. I had one of those crescent roll biscuit things. I opened two cans of that and those mini weenies and we just started making little pigs in the blankets before gift opening.

Scotty McCreery

PLATINUM SELLING RECORDING ARTIST AND WINNER OF THE 10TH SEASON OF *AMERICAN IDOL*

We don't really have any crazy Christmas traditions but we always go to our Christmas Eve service at First Baptist Church in my hometown, Garner, North Carolina. That's just a given. That's the church I grew up in. I always sang in the choir—and one year I was Joseph in the play. After church, we read the Christmas story before bed, or sometimes we read it before we open the presents on Christmas morning. It depends on how tired we are Christmas Eve. I think the part of the story that kills me is that there was no room for Him in the inn. If they only knew Who that baby was and what He was going to mean to this world, I think they probably could have made room!

When it comes to the Christmas story, the people I think I can relate to the most are the shepherds. They were very unassuming, taking care of their flocks in the middle of the night when all of a sudden, "Boom!" there's a star and an angel telling them to go see the Savior. They had to be pretty shocked. They were probably like, "What in the world's going on? We're going to follow a star and see what's going on." I bet that was a pretty amazing sight for the shepherds.

Jesus came into the world so humble and that was the way He was throughout everything. He was the Son of God, but He came in humble beginnings, right down to a manger filled with hay. Any other king would come in and have the whole world know—and they'd certainly be staying in

ht: Scotty opening
s on Christmas.
right: Scotty
tured with Santa
d sister Ashley.

the best place. But there is Jesus with a bunch of animals around Him in a manger. It's pretty cool to see that He comes from those humble beginnings and ended up being the Savior.

Celebrating the birth of our Savior and spending time with family is what Christmas is all about for the McCreerys. On Christmas morning, when we wake up, my sister, Ashley, gets her presents in green and mine come wrapped in red. Santa has always done it that way. I don't know about everybody else, but that's how he does it in the McCreery house. When we were younger we'd always stay in the same room and just count down with the clock because we wanted to get up as early as possible. We'd go downstairs and knock on our parents' door and they'd say, "Too early. Go back to bed!" And we'd go back up for another hour and then come back down. Santa Claus still comes and puts my presents in red and Ashley's in green, and he brings some stuff for the dogs, too. He's still coming around.

My granddaddy gave me my first guitar when I was ten and I had no clue what I was doing with that thing at first. I was just going around strumming it, but that got me into guitar lessons, which led me to singing out and about. That first guitar sparked the public singing outside of church.

> **MY GRANDADDY HAD NO IDEA AT FIRST HOW HIS CHRISTMAS GIFT WOULD CHANGE MY LIFE.**

My granddaddy had no idea at first how his Christmas gift would change my life. I got to sing for him quite a bit as I grew up so he got to see what his little Christmas gift turned into.

After opening presents, I always enjoy going to see both sets of grandparents at Christmas. One set lives on the East Coast and the other set lives in the hills in North Carolina. Christmas was always cool at both places. In Eastern North Carolina, my grandma is very country and they do Christmas the old fashioned way. Then you have my Puerto Rican grandmother Paquita—it's a whole different ballgame for her. She's all about the celebration! There's lots of tinsel on the trees and her decorations are more flamboyant. She has trains running around the tree and bubble machines and stuff. Her personality is big so at Christmas the holiday is like that at her place.

While there are so many things that make Christmas fun, it's important to me that people remember the reason for the season. Nowadays in the commercials, and more and more in the movies, you see less and less of Christ and His birth and the reason we celebrate Christmas. That's why on my Christmas record we have plenty of songs about why the Christmas season is all about the birth of our Savior. I feel it's important for a guy like me who's on a platform to share that Good News with the world.

"When the angels had left them and gone into heaven, the shepherds said to one another, 'Let's go to Bethlehem and see this thing that has happened, which the Lord has told us about.' So they hurried off and found Mary and Joseph, and the baby, who was lying in the manger."

Luke 2:15–16

FAVORITE CHRISTMAS RECIPE

MAMA'S BREAKFAST PIE

Serves 8

There's sausage, and eggs, and cheese—and she'll try to hide some healthy stuff in there too without us knowing. Breakfast pie is always part of our Christmas morning. Oh, and Pillsbury cinnamon rolls have been part of Christmas morning for me a long time, too.

INGREDIENTS

1 roll (12 ounces) breakfast sausage

2 cups shredded Cheddar cheese

6 eggs, beaten

1 cup water

1/2 cup milk

1 package McCormick® Original Country Gravy Mix Substitutions

6 slices bread, cut into 1-inch cubes

Paprika

DIRECTIONS

Preheat oven to 325°F. Cook crumbled sausage in large skillet on medium heat until brown, stirring occasionally. Drain sausage. Spread in lightly greased 11x7-inch baking dish. Sprinkle cheese over sausage. Beat eggs, water, milk and gravy mix in medium bowl with wire whisk until well blended. Pour over cheese. Arrange bread cubes evenly over mixture. Drizzle butter over bread, if desired. Sprinkle with paprika. Bake, uncovered, 40 minutes or until knife inserted in center comes out clean. Let stand 10 minutes before serving.

ie Daniels's career has spanned five decades and multiple genres. As a songwriter, Elvis Presley rded his work. As a musician, Bob Dylan tapped him to play guitar on such landmark albums as *Nashville ne*. Best known for his classic hit "The Devil Went Down to Georgia," Daniels is a Grammy winner and has multiple awards from the Gospel Music Association, Country Music Association, and Academy of Country ic. Daniels is a member of the Grand Ole Opry and has been named a BMI Icon.

Charlie

DANIELS

Below Left: Charlie plays Santa
Bottom: Charlie Daniels Parade of Trees

Photo: Courtesy Charlie Daniels

Photo: Courtesy Danielle DiGregorio

Photo: Courtesy Charlie Daniels

Growing up in North Carolina, Christmas was always such an exciting time for us kids. When I start talking about Christmas, I have so many early memories. In the pre-knowing about Santa Claus days, that's magic time. That's the time of child-like faith. There's nothing like it. It's a great time in a kid's life.

After I grew up and began traveling as a musician, there were times I couldn't be home for Christmas. Back before Hazel and I were married, I remember one Christmas I didn't go home because I had one day off in Wichita, Kansas. I spent Christmas going to a movie that year. Even after we were married, I was on the road two Christmases. After my son, Charlie Jr., was born, that was especially hard.

When it gets close to Christmas time, the Christmas carols start playing and they're showing Rudolph the Red Nosed Reindeer on TV—you can't help but get homesick. I mean just really, really homesick. I probably value my time home with the family during Christmas more than a lot of people do who never had to spend Christmas away from home.

Photo: Courtesy Charlie Daniels

I PROBABLY VALUE *my time home with the family during* CHRISTMAS MORE THAN A LOT OF PEOPLE DO WHO NEVER HAD TO SPEND IT *away from home.*

My favorite night of the year is Christmas Eve. We go to church for a special Christmas service. Afterward, we have folks over for some food and some wine, and fellowship. Then, on Christmas Day, we open our gifts on Christmas morning. Charlie Jr. comes down and we get together, usually with about twenty-five people, for Christmas dinner. It's our tradition. I love the things that you do year after year.

Every Christmas Eve, I read St. Luke's version of the Christmas story. A while back I wrote a book that had some short stories in it. One was called "Carolina Christmas Carol." Years ago, Charlie said, "Daddy, why don't you read that on Christmas Eve night?" So I did and it's become one of our traditions. Every Christmas Eve, I read that and St. Luke's version of the Christmas story.

One of my favorite Christmas memories was in 1967. Those days were pretty much hand-to-mouth for us. I was doing anything I could to make a living. I was going up to Lexington, Kentucky, every Friday

Above: At Grandaddy's house with dogs.

Photo: Courtesy Charlie Daniels

and Saturday to work at a bowling alley. Hazel had joined a bowling league in our neighborhood, but we couldn't afford a bowling ball for her. So I did a little extra work in Lexington and went and bought her a bowling ball. I said nothing to her about it until I gave it to her on Christmas morning. She's still got it after all these years—probably the most meaningful gift that I ever gave because it was something she did not expect at all. It really touched her heart and it touched mine to see her appreciate it so much.

When it comes to the Christmas story, the characters I most identify with are the shepherds. They were, from what I understand, the bottom of the food chain. They weren't looked on very highly as members of society. God's Son could have been born anywhere, but it was not in a royal palace, or a rich man's house, but of all places, a stable. And who got the news first?

The most humble people—the shepherds.

Can you imagine what it would have been like if you're just out in the field all day, and all of a sudden the sky lights up, and a bunch of angels come and tell you to get on your way because the Messiah that you had been waiting on for thousands of years was born? Can you imagine what that must have been like to see the Messiah as a baby lying in a manger? It's just pretty awesome to think that actually happened.

CHARLIE & HAZEL DANIELS' CHRISTMAS MENU

Turkey
Gravy
Mashed potatoes
Green beans or turnip greens
Pumpkin pie w/whipped cream

Cornbread dressing
Yeast rolls
Sweet potatoes
Cranberry salad

FAVORITE CHRISTMAS RECIPE

SWEET POTATO DISH

INGREDIENTS
3 cups sweet potatoes cooked and mashed
1 cup sugar
2 eggs beaten
1 teaspoon vanilla
⅓ cup milk

DIRECTIONS
Mix all ingredients together; place in baking dish sprayed with Pam.

TOPPING INGREDIENTS
1 cup brown sugar
½ cup flour
½ cup butter softened
¾ cup chopped pecans

DIRECTIONS
Mix together and then spread on top of potatoes. Bake 25 minutes at 350° F until browned. Watch your time; you don't want to dry out the potatoes.

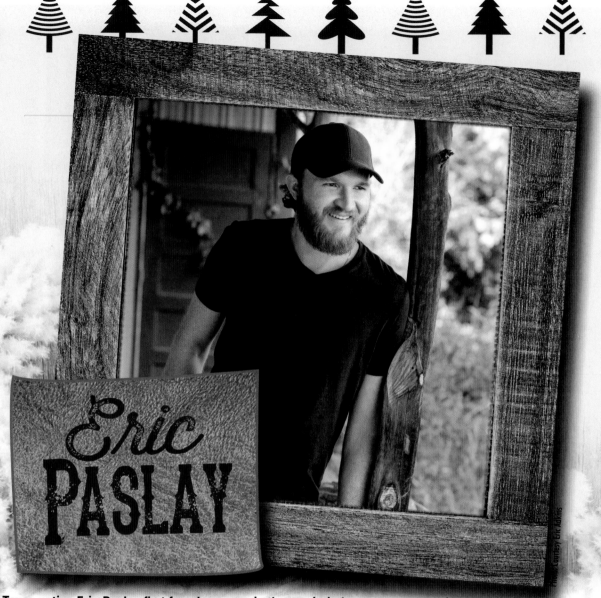

Photo courtesy Eric Adkins

Texas native Eric Paslay first found success in the music industry as a songwriter, penning such hits as Jake Owen's "Barefoot Blue Jean Night" and the Eli Young Band's "Even If It Breaks Your Heart." These days, Eric has also become known as a recording artist in his own right, scoring his first No. 1 with the hit "Friday Night" and following it up with the poignant "She Don't Love You."

Growing up, we would always make the journey on Christmas from our house in Waco, Texas, to my grandma's house in my mom's hometown of Temple, Texas. Where grandmother lives, everyone decorates their house to the nines with Christmas lights. The entire neighborhood gets into the spirit of things. There were carolers, carriage rides through the neighborhood, cars traveling slowly to see all the lights and decorations. It was really special.

Since all my relatives lived in the same neighborhood, we'd start at Grandma's house with dinner and then walk back and forth to my aunt's and uncles' houses to continue the celebration. My family enjoys opening gifts earlier, so we'll open Christmas gifts on Christmas Eve with my mom's family, and then on Christmas morning with my dad's side of the family. On Christmas Eve, our family goes to the Christmas Eve service at church and then we head to my grandma's house for dinner and to frantically open all the Christmas gifts.

As kids, we were blessed to have a few gifts to open growing up. I remember drinking from Santa Claus cups throughout the season. I've held on to a few of them, which I still have today. The first instrument I ever got was a tenor ukulele as a Christmas gift from my grandmother and my parents. Considering where my life has gone, it was such a special gift. The most memorable gifts throughout my

Photo: Courtesy Eric Paslay

life have been musical instruments because they are still around in my life today.

Church plays a huge role in our Christmas celebration. One of my favorite memories as a kid was making the journey from our house to see my grandmother. For the entire thirty-mile drive, I was looking out the window trying to find the Star of Bethlehem. I expected it to show up in the sky every

Christmas! I learned when I was six years old that it only appeared in the sky when Jesus was born.

At different times in our lives we can be all kinds of characters in the Christmas story. Sometimes as parents we're shepherds leading children, or as musicians on stage playing that one song trying to help the lost get found. There are times where you feel like Joseph and Mary following an angel sent from God trying to get you on the right path. Sometimes we are the innkeeper trying to give as much as we can to people even if we're out of room.

I would say I most closely identify with the wise men though because they journey and travel so far to see if Jesus is really there. I know Jesus is really there, but I feel like a traveler following the star of music. I'm glad that God lets me follow music. I don't want to be the star—I just want to be the one singing about the Star.

MOM'S CHRISTMAS COCONUT NOODLES

From my mom Donna Paslay

INGREDIENTS
1 package medium egg noodles
butter
sugar
coconut
cinnamon

DIRECTIONS
Boil medium egg noodles until firm and done (not too soft). If you can find RONCO noodles, they are the best! Drain just a little bit. Add butter and sugar to taste, then pour into glass casserole dish. In separate small skillet, sauté some butter and coconut until coconut starts turning medium brown, then pour over top of noodles. Sprinkle cinnamon and sugar on top.

Magi from the east came to
JERUSALEM
AND ASKED,
"WHERE IS THE ONE WHO HAS BEEN BORN
King OF THE *Jews?"*
WE SAW HIS STAR WHEN IT ROSE AND HAVE
COME TO WORSHIP HIM.

Matthew 2:1b, 2

Photo: Courtesy Nikki Hollis

Phil VASSAR

A native of Lynchburg, Virginia, Phil Vassar began his career penning hits for Collin Raye, Tim McGraw, and Alan Jackson, among others. He was named ASCAP's Country Songwriter of the Year in 1999, the same year he signed a recording deal with Arista Nashville. He's released eight critically acclaimed albums, spawning such chart-topping hits as "Just Another Day in Paradise" and "In a Real Love." He currently records for his own label, Rodeowave Entertainment.

When I was growing up in Virginia, we were pretty poor people. We didn't have a lot of stuff, but Christmas was an exciting time and my favorite holiday. Our parents scraped together whatever they could to get what we wanted. I love Christmas because it's the time of year when everything winds down and everyone puts their priorities in their life into perspective by focusing on what's really important. I wish every day was like that. If we did, we'd probably all be okay.

Being with family was a big part of our Christmas celebration. Our tradition was to split our time between our grandmothers' houses. It was about the food and who's cooking this and that. My grandparents would come over in the morning, then we would go back over there to one of their houses for lunch. And then for dinner we'd go to the other house. Of course, you're as full as a tick by the time it's over with as you waddle home. It was so good. I miss that. Both of my grandmothers are gone now. And we're all split up all over the country, so I try to get everybody to come to Nashville now.

I love **CHRISTMAS BECAUSE IT'S THE TIME OF YEAR WHEN** *Everything* **WINDS DOWN AND** *Everyone* **PUTS THEIR PRIORITIES IN THEIR LIFE INTO** *perspective.*

I've got two younger sisters. My baby sisters are two and six years younger than I am. There was lots of girl stuff going on around our house. That's what I grew up with. My dad was gone a long, long time ago, so it's always been me and the girls. And now I have two daughters so it's the same thing. It never changes—me spaced out in the estrogen pool of life. Still, Christmas Eve is our thing. We read the Christmas story and "'Twas the Night Before Christmas" before we open presents and have dinner on Christmas Eve.

Everybody comes back over for breakfast Christmas morning. I'm the one who cooks the breakfast. I used to have a restaurant, so I know how to cook a little bit. I'm not going to say I'm some chef or anything, but I can work up some eggs and bacon like nobody's business. Afterward, me and my girls drink hot chocolate and watch *A Christmas Story* and *Christmas Vacation*.

The first gift I remember getting was a set of drums. I don't know if you should ever give your kid a set of drums. You're just asking for it, especially in an eight-hundred-square-foot house—maybe even smaller. One day my drums just disappeared. I said, "Where did that drum set go?" I think my parents just said, "Okay, that was dumb." When I was older, someone gave me a painting of me and my girls which is still in my house. That's one of my favorite gifts I've ever received. When somebody brings a painting of your girls to you, that's a pretty cool thing.

Ultimately, Christmas always comes back to Jesus. It just comes back to that. It's gotten so commercialized these days. When I'm with my family and it's Christmas, it's like the world goes away and we're in our own little universe. I love that. I also think about that first Christmas. If I had to pick one of the characters, I'm definitely one of the shepherds watching over their flock by night. I think that would probably be me—hanging out with my iPhone, checking my emails, watching my flock.

PUMPKIN BREAD

INGREDIENTS
3 ½ cups flour
1 ½ teaspoons salt
2 teaspoons baking soda
1 teaspoon cinnamon
1 teaspoon nutmeg
3 cups sugar
1 cup oil
⅔ cup water
4 eggs, beaten
2 cups pumpkin
1 cup chopped nuts (optional)

DIRECTIONS
Sift flour, salt, soda, spices, and sugar together into a mixing bowl. Add oil, water, eggs, and pumpkin, beat until smooth. Stir in nuts; turn batter into 3 greased and lightly floured 1-pound loaf pans. Fill pans half full and bake at 350° F for 1 hour. Cool before removing from pan.

Left: Phil Vassar. Right: Jimmy Howard, Phil Vassar, and sister Terri Vassar.

*When the angels had left them
and gone into heaven*

THE SHEPHERDS

SAID TO ONE ANOTHER,

LET'S GO TO BETHLEHEM

AND SEE THIS THING THAT HAS HAPPENED,

WHICH THE *Lord* HAS TOLD US ABOUT.

Luke 2:15

Spotlighted by Country Music Television (CMT) as one of the Next Women of Country, this Rossville, Georgia, native is well known for her powerhouse vocals and effervescent personality. She was the first runner up on the tenth season of *American Idol* when she was just sixteen years old, and soon after launched her recording career with the debut album *Wildflower*.

Lauren ALAINA

Photo: Courtesy Joseph Llanes

My family loved to put up decorations for Christmas every year—and we still do. When we were kids, my mom made sure she put a pretty tree upstairs and let my brother and I decorate the "crazy tree" downstairs. Admittedly, our tree wasn't very pretty but we had a blast decorating it each year. And, every Christmas Eve our tradition included going to our church for a midnight candle lighting to celebrate Jesus' birth. We wanted to make sure to start the day with its true meaning.

The person I most identify with in the Christmas story is Joseph because even though he and Mary were turned away at the inn, he still found a place to keep them safe. I think family is so important and, like Joseph, I would do anything to keep my family safe.

Today, my new tradition is to go caroling—which has quickly topped my list of favorite things to do every year. Like my good friend Buddy the Elf says, "The best way to spread Christmas cheer, is singing loud for all to hear." I'll never forget the time we went caroling where we sang at this lady's house. Afterward, she looked at me and suggested that I try out for *American Idol*. Everyone in our group of carolers burst out laughing—which confused her. I explained that I didn't think I could win and that, at best, I would get second or something. But she insisted I would win. It was hilarious.

As much as I love getting gifts for Christmas, I love giving them even more. Shopping and picking out just the right thing for every person I love is probably my favorite thing. The excitement little kids get when they open their gifts is the kind of excitement I get when I see someone open a gift I've picked out for them.

When I was twelve years old, my mom got me a custom-made, pink, brown, and white Bible personalized with my name on the front. That's the one gift that I've held closest to my heart. It's the first Bible that I took time to really read and understand the Word. I love that gift because it reflects what's truly important to me about Christmas—not receiving gifts, but receiving Jesus.

Left: Lauren and boyfriend Alex Hopkins caroling. Below: Lauren's childhood Christmas.

Photos: Courtesy Lauren Alaina

FAVORITE CHRISTMAS RECIPE

NANA'S SUGAR COOKIES

INGREDIENTS

2 ¾ cups all-purpose flour
1 teaspoon baking soda
½ teaspoon baking powder
1 cup softened butter
1 ½ cups sugar
1 egg
1 teaspoon vanilla extract

DIRECTIONS

Stir together flour, baking soda, and baking powder. Cream butter and sugar and beat in the egg and vanilla. Then blend in the flour mixture. Roll into balls and drop onto an ungreased cookie sheet. Bake 8–10 minutes at 375° F.

Let cool before frosting and decorating. Be creative!

Photo: Joseph L. Lanes

Lee BRICE

A compelling vocalist and insightful songwriter, this Sumpter, South Carolina, native has sold more than 1.2 million albums and over nine million singles. He's earned numerous industry honors and five No. 1 hits, including "I Drive Your Truck"—named Song of the Year by both the Country Music Association (CMA) and Academy of Country Music (ACM). His chart-topping hit "I Don't Dance" was named Single of the Year at the 2015 ACMs.

On Christmas Eve we would always go to church and afterward we would go to my grandmother's on my daddy's side, my grandmother Brice. Our extended family would be at my grandmother's house where Granddaddy would cook a pig. Then my daddy, my mama, my brother, and I would spend Christmas morning together. Santa would come and we'd tip toe through the house trying not to wake up Mama and Daddy too early to peek at our gifts.

The Saturday after Christmas is when we would meet on my mama's side of the family. We'd go to Aunt Floranna's house or sometimes to Aunt Lori's—short for Loretta—and play football, ride four wheelers, open presents, and hang out. It was our tradition. I miss those days. I haven't been able to go back home in years. I spend Christmas in Nashville with my family—which is great, but it's different not being able to get back there. The schedule now in my life is so busy. There's a lot of sacrifice to be able to do this music career.

From Our Family to Yours Have a Beautiful Christmas And a Happy New Year.

A Brice family Christmas card.

Still, my family is so important to me. One of my favorite Christmas memories involves a visit with my granddaddy. At the time I'd had songs on the radio. I'd been playing my whole life but for some reason I'd never sat down and played for my granddaddy. I knew he was always so proud of me, seeing me on TV and at concerts. So one Christmas Eve my brother and I brought our guitars over. With the whole family gathered together, we took turns playing and we also played together with granddaddy sitting there.

As we played, I remember the look on his face. He was so overjoyed. He was visibly emotional. Even though his health was fading, to see him that happy was so special. Shortly after that, he passed away. I just think, "What if I hadn't done that?" It would have been one of those things that you regret you didn't do. It's the last memory I have of my granddaddy before he was gone.

When I was a kid one of the most memorable gifts I got was a football—a big, official-size football, not a little kid football. I had that football for so many years. That had such an influence on me to become a big football fan my whole life and really driving to be a football player. Now that I have kids, it's important to me to instill in them what Christmas is really all about. Because it's easy to get carried away at Christmas, we only do three presents for my son—one present that he needs, one present that reminds him of what Christmas is about, and then one present that he wants. It's hard to not get lots of gifts, but first I want him to be appreciative of everything he has and to remember what Christmas is all about.

When I, as a daddy, think about the Christmas story, the character I feel closest to is Joseph. I think of how he must have felt in his position,

being a daddy to a little boy. That feeling having your first son, there's nothing like it.

FAVORITE CHRISTMAS RECIPE

GRANDMA DOT'S MAC & CHEESE

This was passed down to my wife and I from my mother Carlleen Brice who got it from my paternal grandmother Dot Brice. It's as delicious today as when Grandma used to make it.

INGREDIENTS
1 box of noodles
1 can Carnation milk
½ stick butter
3 eggs, beaten
½ cup sharp cheddar cheese
½ cup mild cheddar cheese
¼ cup mayonnaise

Lee gets a thank-you from wife Sara.

Photo: Courtesy Lee Brice

DIRECTIONS
Start by preheating the oven to 350° F. Boil noodles 13 minutes. Strain and then place in casserole dish. Blend all ingredients and then add the carnation milk to make soupy. Bake for 20 minutes.

For God so loved the world

that he gave his one and only

Son,

that whoever believes in him

shall not

perish

but have eternal life.

John 3:16

FLORIDA GEORGIA Line

Photo: Courtesy Jeremy Cowart

When a former worship leader from Georgia met an aspiring baseball player from Florida at Nashville's Belmont University, the creative sparks exploded into country music's most successful new act. Georgia-born Tyler Hubbard and Florida native Brian Kelley have earned numerous accolades and scored seven (and counting) No. 1 hits, including their breakout single "Cruise," which set a record as the bestselling country digital song of all time—with sales surpassing 7 million copies, and spent twenty-four weeks at No. 1 on Billboard's country singles chart, setting a record for the longest chart-topper.

Tyler HUBBARD

We usually just enjoy some time off with family at Christmas. I think that's the most important thing, and we try to give back during the holiday season. We really find a lot of joy in that. Helping others means a lot to us because we've been in a spot before when we didn't have anything to give, so it feels good to have something to give—especially doing that during the Christmas season when not everybody has what they need. The Christmas holiday is also great because we have a little down time, a little recharge time, a little family time, and we love being home!

When I think about the characters in the Christmas story, I think the wise men are the people we can most relate to because we are always chasing a star and chasing where the Lord wants us to go. That's a cool part of the story.

Photos: Courtesy Tyler Hubbard

Top: Tyler Hubbard, Cameron Hubbard, Santa, Amy Hubbard, Amelia Hubbard, and Roy Hubbard. Bottom: Roy Hubbard, Tyler Hubbard, Amy Hubbard, and Cameron Hubbard.

Brian KELLEY

I agree with Tyler. It's all about spending time with family and giving back at Christmas. We don't get to see our family as much as we'd like throughout the year because we're gone and working, doing our thing. At Christmas, we try to get together with family, just sit back, and be thankful for what we have—and that, in turn, turns into giving back, whether that's our time, our resources, or helping people out.

As far as a favorite character from the Christmas story, I can definitely relate to the wise men, too. You know, just continuing to chase the path God wants us to be on. We're doing that for sure. That's what we're all about. I'd have to say my favorite Christmas song is "Mary Did You Know?" We both love the perspective of that song.

FLORIDA GEORGIA Line

FAVORITE CHRISTMAS RECIPE

FANTASY FUDGE
Makes 3 pounds

This recipe was handed down in Tyler Hubbard's family for years. It's a perennial favorite. I don't know why we never make it any other time of year!

Prep Time: 10 minutes   Total Time: 22 minutes

INGREDIENTS
1 ½ sticks butter or margarine, softened
3 cups sugar
1 5-ounce can evaporated milk (⅔ cup)
12 ounces semi-sweet chocolate chips
1 7-ounce jar Marshmallow Crème
1 teaspoon vanilla
1 cup pecans

DIRECTIONS
Microwave butter in 4-quart microwavable bowl on HIGH 1 minute or until melted. Add sugar and milk; mix well. Microwave 5 minutes or until mixture begins to boil, stirring after 3 minutes. Stir well, scraping down sides of bowl. Microwave 5 ½ minutes, stirring after 3 minutes. Let stand 2 minutes.
Add chocolate; stir until melted. Add Marshmallow Crème and vanilla; mix well. Stir in nuts.
Pour into greased 13 x 9 inch pan.
Cool at room temperature; cut into squares.

THE ANGEL ANSWERED,
"*The Holy Spirit will come on you,*
and the power of the
MOST HIGH,
WILL OVERSHADOW YOU.
SO THE HOLY ONE TO BE BORN
WILL BE CALLED
Son of God.

Luke 1:35

Mickey GUYTON

Texas native Mickey Guyton is rapidly earning a reputation as one of country music's most talented new singer/songwriters and gaining fans with her first single "Better than You Left Me." Even before the release of her self-titled EP, Guyton made her TV debut performing at the White House for President Obama on a PBS TV special that included Kris Kristofferson, James Taylor, Darius Rucker, and Alison Krauss. She's spent much of 2015 opening for Brad Paisley on his "Crushin' It World Tour."

Every Christmas morning when my family wakes up, we drink orange juice and read the story of Jesus's birth. Then we pray and open gifts. After gifts all of our extended family comes over and we all have Christmas dinner together. One year we did a Christmas play that we made up in fifteen minutes. It was pretty funny. I personally don't have any traditions myself because I don't have a family yet but I'm planning on carrying on my childhood traditions with my own family someday.

Church plays a major role in my Christmas celebration. If Christmas is on a Sunday, we go to church in the morning and then open presents. If I don't make it home early enough to go to church with my family, I always try to go to a candlelight service on Christmas Eve.

I'm really bad at asking for presents but one year I asked for an iPad because I didn't have a computer and couldn't afford one. This was around the time I had first moved to Nashville. I had to go to writing sessions and would have to write songs on my phone. Every time I would go to a writing session I would always have to explain that I was writing the songs on my phone—and not texting or surfing the internet. When Christmas came around I opened my gift: it was a Mac laptop! My dad told me he wanted me to look professional when I went in to my writing sessions. I couldn't believe my parents bought that for me! It was so awesome and thoughtful.

The character from the Christmas story that I'd have to say I most closely identify with is the innkeeper. I don't have much but whatever I have I don't mind sharing with people up to the last penny or space in my little apartment. At times it is really hard, but God always seems to keep blessing me for it. Like Jesus says, "It is better to give than to receive."

Photo: Courtesy Mickey Guyton

FAVORITE CHRISTMAS RECIPE

BLUEBERRY DUMP CAKE

INGREDIENTS
¾ cup butter, plus more for dish
1 20-ounce can crushed pineapple, in juice
1 20-ounce can blueberry pie filling
1 18.25-ounce box yellow cake mix
1 cup chopped pecans

DIRECTIONS
Preheat oven to 350° F. Butter a 13 x 9 inch casserole dish. Melt ¾ cup butter in saucepan over low heat. Pour the pineapple with juice into the casserole dish and evenly spread blueberry pie filling on top. Cover with dry yellow cake mix and top with pecans. Drizzle with melted butter and bake for 35–45 minutes.

Wade HAYES

A native of Bethel Acres, Oklahoma, Wade Hayes hit the top of the chart with his first single, "Old Enough to Know Better," and continued to serve up such top ten hits as "I'm Still Dancing with You," "What I Meant to Say," "The Day She Left Tulsa (In a Chevy)," and "On a Good Night." Surviving colon cancer twice inspired the title track of Hayes's latest album, Go Live Your Life, and when he's not recording and touring, he helps raise money and awareness to battle colon cancer.

Photo: Courtesy Angelynn Tinsley

We always did Christmas a little bit different. We would open presents from our parents on Christmas Eve and then go to bed. Then, we'd get the Santa Claus gifts on Christmas morning. My very favorite Christmas by far is when I was eleven years old and I got my first guitar. On this last album, *Go Live Your Life*, I played that guitar on the last track. It's been through my cousins who had it for a while. When I got it back two years ago, I got it back from Mom and Dad and it was beat up pretty bad. I put it in the shop and they got it back to being semi-playable.

One of my favorite things about Christmas is my mom's Christmas fudge. That's the only time of year that we had the fudge and I loved it. We had stockings at the fireplace and it was kind of your typical Christmas. As I got older, I kind of got out of the Christmas spirit because it got commercialized and it didn't mean the same to me. It has totally gotten away from the true meaning, especially

how that we say "Happy Holidays" instead of "Merry Christmas." That really is a sticking point with me.

When it comes to the Christmas story, I identify with the Wise Men. They were searching for the Savior and that's something I've been doing my whole life and, for the longest time, I didn't understand it. I can remember when I sincerely started looking and trying to find answers. I was about eighteen or nineteen years old and knew that there was something in the meaning of Christmas that I didn't understand, but I knew I wanted. I didn't have a grasp on it. I've always had a heart for that, but I didn't understand it.

It's weird how you can grow up in church and not understand the significance of Christmas. I think a lot of people are in that boat. After I moved to Nashville, I got into a Bible study group with Bill Simpson, this fellow from Georgia who is very, very knowledgeable about the Bible. We went through it line by line and I finally started understanding what it was all about—the need for Jesus and the reason He had to do what He did and the reason we are hopeless without Him.

I try to do a Bible study every day that I can, and I'll go to church every Sunday that I'm home. It's more important to me now that I've gotten older and understand that need for Jesus. I found that my life goes so much better when I'm in the Word and when I'm trying to walk in what the Bible teaches and keep it on my heart and mind. When I get away from it, I notice things start falling apart.

FAVORITE CHRISTMAS RECIPE

OLD FASHION FUDGE

Makes about 2 pounds of candy. I always double the recipe—it's that good!

INGREDIENTS
2/3 cup evaporated milk
1 cup sugar
¼ teaspoon salt
¼ cup butter
16 marshmallows, or 1 jar (5 to 10 ounces) marshmallow cream
1½ cups semi-sweet chocolate pieces
1 teaspoon vanilla
1 cup walnuts or pecans chopped or broken—I always used pecans in mine.

DIRECTIONS
Mix first 5 ingredients together and bring to a boil stirring constantly. Boil 5 minutes stirring constantly. Remove from heat. Add chocolate pieces and stir until melted. Stir in vanilla and nuts. Spread in buttered 8 inch pan. Cool until firm.

ELI YOUNG Band

The Eli Young Band launched their career by building a strong fan base in their native Texas and then gained national success when they signed with Republic Records. They hit No. 1 with "Crazy Girl," which won Song of the Year from the Academy of Country Music in 2012. They since scored two more No. 1 hits, including "Even If It Breaks Your Heart," which has been certified platinum.

Mike ELI

(Eli Young Band)

Above: Mike's first Christmas.
Below: Mike poses for a Christmas keepsake.

I grew up in the Houston area. In that part of Texas, rarely do you ever get snow—it's always ice or sleet. But one Christmas, I don't remember the year, we woke up and there was just a little snow on the ground. Not ice, real white powder sitting there. That was the only white Christmas we had in Texas growing up.

Each year when we woke up on Christmas morning, Santa's presents were never wrapped. I thought that was the natural thing because the gifts from Santa were never wrapped. Now that we've got a little one at home, it's really fun to have that night before when you set up the toys in front of the tree. Then, when she walks around the corner, she sees everything sitting out from Santa, unwrapped.

There was one year when my parents were financially going through some hard times. They didn't really have any money for Christmas gifts so my mom entered a raffle at a Texaco to win a Texaco go-cart. It had a fiberglass body and looked great! Right before Christmas she got a call saying that we had won the go-cart. It was sitting in the living room on Christmas morning, which was pretty neat—especially since they didn't have any money to get my sister and I anything.

Church played a big part in our Christmas celebration. I grew up Catholic so we went to Christmas Mass. As you grow up, you appreciate it a little more than you probably did when you were younger—you realize the things you should be thankful for.

Photos: Courtesy Eli Young Band

Chris THOMPSON

(Eli Young Band)

The most exciting thing for me about Christmas is the music at the Christmas Eve service. One of our traditions has been to pick a musical event—whether it's seeing the Nutcracker, or watching a choir perform in the Christmas season. That way we kind of combined the religious and the entertainment side of the holiday together.

Jon JONES

(Eli Young Band)

I love the music of Christmas. We'll go to concerts leading up to Christmas and we'll go to the Christmas Eve late night service to hear the hand bell choir. One year I missed all of the Christmas fun because I had chickenpox. I didn't get to go to any of the festivities. My mom had to stay home with me the whole time. It was a bummer.

Photos on pages 66 and 67: Courtesy Eli Young Band

James YOUNG

(Eli Young Band)

My parents would always hide the big present in the garage or in the backyard. We used to go find our presents. When I was ten years old, I got my first electric guitar. That was probably the most meaningful gift I got for Christmas as a kid. Now that I'm older, there's nothing more powerful than going to the Christmas Eve service, hearing and singing carols; it really puts you into the reason why you celebrate the holiday. When it comes to a character in the Christmas story, I probably identify most with the innkeeper. I hope that we would all be generous and open our doors to people.

CHOCOLATE DELIGHT

Eli Young Band Favorite Recipe

1st LAYER INGREDIENTS
1 ½ cups flour
1 ½ sticks margarine, melted
2 tablespoons sugar
1 cup pecans
DIRECTIONS Mix together, press into 13x9 inch dish. Bake at 350°F for 20 minutes.

2ND LAYER INGREDIENTS
1 cup cool whip (14-ounce carton)
1 cup powdered sugar
8-ounce package cream cheese
DIRECTIONS Mix on low speed until fluffy. Spread on cooled crust.

3RD LAYER INGREDIENTS
Mix Together:
1 ½ cups sugar
1 tablespoon (rounded) of cocoa
3 heaping tablespoons cornstarch
½ teaspoon salt
DIRECTIONS
In a separate bowl microwave 4 egg yolks and 3 cups milk for 3 minutes, stir and microwave 3 more minutes. Add to dry ingredients. Add 2 tablespoons butter and 2 teaspoons vanilla. Mix and spread over 2nd layer.

4TH LAYER
Spread remaining cool whip on top and refrigerate 4 hours. Garnish with grated chocolate.

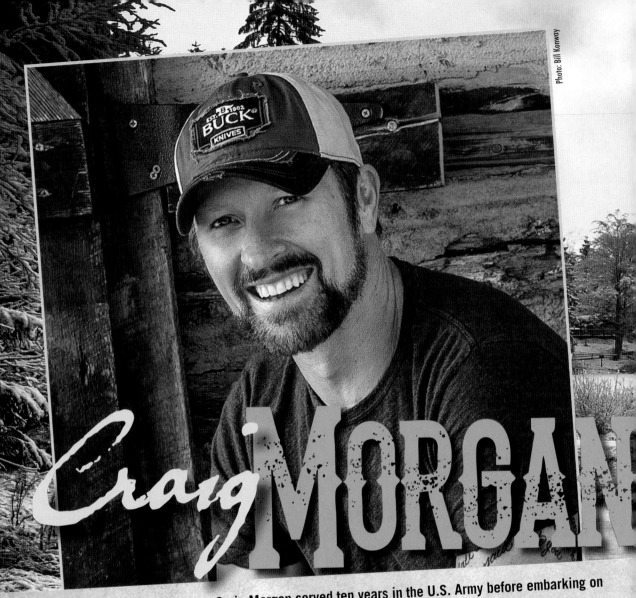

Passionate about God and country, Craig Morgan served ten years in the U.S. Army before embarking on a career in country music. Since inking his first record deal in 2000, Morgan has delivered such hits as "Almost Home," "International Harvester," and "That's What I Love About Sunday"—a chart topper for four weeks and named Billboard's No. 1 Country song of the year in 2005. A member of the Grand Ole Opry, Morgan also hosts his own TV show, *Craig Morgan: All Access Outdoors.*

W hen we were kids, we started celebrating Christmas ten to twelve days out. Each night we were allowed to open up one present until Christmas Eve—at which time we opened what was left under the tree. Then, on Christmas day, Santa Claus came. It's a tradition we have carried forward to our children. But, growing up in a lower middle class family, we didn't have a lot of money so Christmas was important for us because we didn't get stuff throughout the year like my kids do.

When my kids need something, they get it pretty much.

One Christmas my parents had a really good year. Not only did we get the stuff we needed, like clothes and the essentials that we only got at Christmas, but we also got a lot of toys. I was maybe thirteen or fourteen years old at the time and my parents gave me the Remington 20 gauge shotgun to hunt with that I had hoped for. That gun represented that I was becoming a man—at least that's what I thought it represented.

This Christmas I'm looking forward to having Christmas dinner with meat from the smokehouse that my sons and I built on our farm in Dickson, Tennessee. I have a wild, salt-cured ham hanging

Photo: Courtesy Craig Morgan

Craig celebrates the season with family.

there that we plan to reconstitute and cook this year. I tried it once before but I didn't do something right in my process. I think we've got the process down now and are really excited to get a ham that we cured ourselves.

Church doesn't play as big a role as much as our Christian faith. We celebrate Christmas knowing that it represents the birth of our Lord and Savior, Jesus Christ. Church is a place we go—Christians are who we are. Christmas is special to me because it's the time we celebrate the coming of Christ. One thing that other religions don't have is a living God. Our Lord is alive. He awoke from the dead so we worship and celebrate a living God at Christmas.

I love the way God is using my kids to show me how much He loves me. When you think about how much you love your kids, that's the relationship He has with us. It's pretty amazing when you think about all the stuff we do—myself in particular. I look at my life and think, "How can He care about me with the bad things I've done?" But when I look at my children and they do something, it doesn't matter what they've done, I still love them. God's love for us is even greater than that!

When I think about the Christmas story, I most closely identify with the shepherds because they were on time. For me, that's real important. Timing is everything. It's amazing that the shepherds managed to get to where they had to be in perfect timing, and they did that without the resources we have. When my kids and I talk about the Christmas story, I remind them how God has perfect timing. The shepherds epitomize that fact. And in my own life, God's timing has always been perfect. It ain't when I want it . . . it's when I need it—because God knows me better than I know myself.

God's timing is perfect!

DEVILED EGGS

I know this seems like an odd choice for my favorite Christmas recipe, but it's Deviled Eggs. For some reason, my mom always made them at Christmas with the red paprika on top.

INGREDIENTS
6 eggs, hardboiled
¼ cup mayonnaise
1 teaspoon vinegar
1 teaspoon mustard
Pinch salt
Pinch paprika

DIRECTIONS
Remove the shell from the hardboiled eggs; cut in half. Arrange the egg whites cut side up on a serving dish and place the yolks into a medium bowl. Mash the yolks, then add the mayonnaise, vinegar, mustard, and salt. Mix well. Add the yolk mixture to the egg whites, then sprinkle with paprika. Serve chilled.

"The Virgin will conceive
and give birth
TO A SON,
AND THEY WILL CALL HIM
Immanuel"
(WHICH MEANS "GOD WITH US")

Matthew 1:23

Photo: Courtesy Erick Anderson

The ROYS

Siblings Lee and Elaine Roy are known for their skilled musicianship and beautiful harmonies. The duo won Inspirational Country Music's Bluegrass Artist of the Year Award for the fourth consecutive year. They've scored such hits as "Coal Minin' Man," "No More Lonely," and "I Wonder What God's Thinking"— the ICM Inspirational Country Single of the Year in 2012.

ELAINE ROY

Christmas was such a special time around the house. Lee and I were born in Massachusetts but moved to Coal Branch, New Brunswick, Canada, where mom was from. The memories burned into my memory include riding snowmobiles to look for a Christmas tree that we'd cut down on our own, and then decorating it while listening to Christmas carols. Going to Midnight Mass was always very special, too. I sang in the choir and I remember the church being full of life and music and fellowship.

Lee and I always waited until Christmas morning to open our presents but we would go to my Grandpa LeBlanc's house when he was still living. He lived with my aunt and uncle and we would all go to church together and gather after Mass at their house where we'd eat Poutines—one of our favorite French Acadian dishes. They'd open a gift and we were so excited to see what they got.

Church has always played a very big role in our celebration of His birth, which is the reason for the season. To this day I love Midnight Mass. Now we celebrate in Fitchburg, Massachusetts,

Above: Elaine and my Uncle Joe, who is playing the fiddle on Christmas Day at the Roys' parent's home in Fitchburg, Massachusetts.
Below: Lee and Elaine on Christmas day in Massachusetts playing for their family get-together.

where we were born and go to the church we attended when we lived there with our parents. After communion they shut all the lights off and there are candles lit all down the aisle of the church as we sing "Silent Night." It is just so moving. It always brings tears to my eyes cause I feel the presence of the Lord in His house and we celebrate the gift that He is.

Looking back, I remember getting a tape recorder as a kid. When I opened that up Christmas morning I was so excited and overjoyed. It was the first time that I could record myself singing and hear myself back. I thought that was the most awesome thing. I think if I looked hard enough I could find one of those tapes buried somewhere in my treasures! It left a lasting impression on me for sure.

Regarding the Christmas story, I think I would most identify with being a shepherd—probably because they were so humble just faithfully doing what they needed to do. When the angels approached them they were scared—I would be, too! But to be chosen to be given such incredible news that a baby was born called Jesus and that He was sent for all of us, and to be privileged to bring the news, that would be such a high honor.

Lee on drums (a Christmas present), and Uncle Alias playing the guitar on Christmas night in our home in Coal Branch, New Brunswick, Canada.

FAVORITE CHRISTMAS RECIPE

CORN CASSEROLE

INGREDIENTS
1 can cream style corn
8 ounces sour cream
1 egg
1 box corn muffin mix
20 ounces frozen corn
1 stick butter

DIRECTIONS
Preheat oven to 350° F. Mix all ingredients together. Spread into a 9 x 13 inch dish. Bake for an hour and 15 minutes and enjoy!

"BUT YOU,

Bethlehem Ephrathah,

THOUGH YOU ARE SMALL

AMONG THE CLANS OF JUDAH,

OUT OF YOU WILL COME FOR ME

ONE WHO WILL BE RULER OVER

ISRAEL,

WHOSE ORIGINS ARE FROM OF OLD,

from ancient times."

Micah 5:2

This founding Hootie & the Blowfish front man turned country artist's debut album *Learn to Live* was certified platinum; in 2009 he was awarded the CMA New Artist of the Year. He has six No. 1 singles, among them "Don't Think I Don't Think About It," "Alright," and "Come Back Song," and he's recorded five albums including a Christmas record, *Home for the Holidays*.

Darius RUCKER

Photos: Courtesy Darius Rucker

Growing up in Charleston, Christmas was awesome! It was always about our family and our cousins from Virginia getting together. You didn't always get all the things you wanted, but you didn't realize it. There was never a Christmas morning that I woke up, didn't get what I wanted, and then pouted about it. I was happy with what I got.

When I was a kid, we made sure we either went to be with family, or the family came to us. That was important then. Still is. So at some point on Christmas, before noon, I'll pack up my wife, Beth, and the kids in the car and go see my sisters and my brothers and my nieces and nephews every year. Christmas is laid back for us. I love that we just sit around and talk, because I travel so much I don't get to see them as much as I want to.

We're a Christmas morning family. Somebody always comes down way too early. It never fails. It will be 3:30 a.m. and somebody comes down and goes, "Santa Clause has been here!" And I'm like, "Yeah, well you're going back to bed for another two hours." We usually get up around 5:30 a.m. and start opening presents. It's all about sitting around and videotaping the kids opening their presents and capturing their reactions. Then we'll have a nice breakfast, put on Christmas music, or watch a Christmas parade on TV. Afterward we'll visit my family for a bit and then come home so the kids can play with whatever they got.

> WHEN I WROTE, "WHAT GOD WANTS FOR CHRISTMAS" THAT WAS A PART OF ME TRYING TO TAKE CHRISTMAS BACK FOR WHAT IT'S REALLY ABOUT.

Growing up, music played a big part in our Christmas celebration. We listened to everything. My favorite of all time was the Temptations Christmas record. I still play that record at my house to this day. That was the ultimate staple of Christmas music in my house growing up. We played records all day on that big hi-fi that we had. Every third record was the Temptations Christmas record. It was such a big part of my life growing up. When I hear "Please Come Home for Christmas" now, I flashback to my mom in the kitchen with my grandma, and Mom singing with the Temptations. I'd be sitting at the table playing cards or something with my cousins while Mom and my aunts were in the kitchen cooking collard greens, okra soup, sweet potato pies, turkey, ham, and macaroni and cheese—all that stuff we love to eat at Christmas down in Charleston. When that song came on and everybody was singing along.

I'm a believer. I know there's a God up there and I thank Him every day for the life He's given me. When I wrote, "What God Wants for Christmas" that was a part of me trying to take Christmas back for what it's really about. Nowadays it's "Happy Holidays." People don't want to say, "Merry Christmas." With that song we broke that mold. Christmas is about the birthday of Jesus Christ, our Lord and Savior. We just wanted to take it back for that three and a half minutes for what it's really about. For me, writing that song just brought out my love of God and my love of Jesus.

Darius's mom Carolyn (center and above).

FAVORITE CHRISTMAS RECIPE

OKRA SOUP   Family Recipe

INGREDIENTS
1 package frozen cut okra
1 large can tomato sauce
1 package frozen whole kernel corn
1 package frozen green Lima beans

You may use smoked neck bones or a ham bone
(purchase from honey ham store).
Canned lima beans and corn may also be used.

DIRECTIONS
First boil meat for 30 to 45 minutes.
If using frozen corn and lima beans, add to pot with
tomato sauce, boil for 20 minutes.
Add okra, season with salt and pepper and pinch of
sugar to taste.

Make sure to let meat boil down to low liquid, do not
drain. If using canned corn and Lima beans be sure
to drain before adding to pot. If you want, add pound
of fresh shrimp and simmer 15 minutes.
Serve over white rice

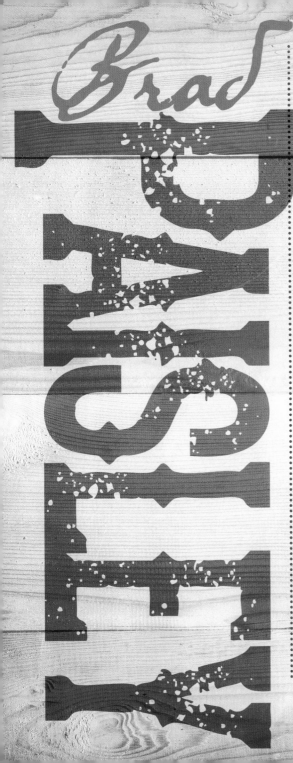

Brad Paisley

MOM SANDY'S WHOLE GRAIN GINGERBREAD

Makes 8 Servings

INGREDIENTS
1 cup whole wheat flour
1 cup unbleached flour
1 teaspoon baking soda
¾ teaspoon salt
1 ½ teaspoon cinnamon
1 teaspoon ginger
¼ teaspoon cloves
¼ cup sugar
½ cup wheat germ
1 cup yogurt or buttermilk
¾ cup molasses
¼ cup applesauce
1 tablespoon oil
2 eggs

Photo: Courtesy Brad Paisley

Brad with parents Sandy and Doug.

DIRECTIONS
Stir dry ingredients (flour through wheat germ) together in a mixing bowl. Add remaining ingredients and beat until smooth. Pour into 9 x 9 inch greased cake pan. Bake at 350° F for 45–50 minutes or until done.
Enjoy warm or cool.

One of Country Music's most talented ambassadors, this West Virginia native has won three Grammys, two American Music Awards, fourteen Academy of Country Music Awards, and fourteen Country Music Association Awards, including Entertainer of the Year. He has written or co-written twenty of his twenty-three No. 1 hits, starting with 1999s "He Didn't Have to Be" and has been a member of the Grand Ole Opry since 2001.

Kimberly SCHLAPMAN

Photo: Courtesy Becky Flukes

A member of the Grammy winning group Little Big Town, Kimberly is well know for her stunning voice and insightful songwriting. Formed in 1998, Little Big Town has won an Emmy, four ACM Awards, and four CMA honors—including Vocal Group of the Year in 2012, 2013, and 2014. Their hit "Girl Crush" spent a record-breaking thirteen consecutive weeks at No. 1. Kimberly hosts her own cooking show, *Simply Southern* and released her first cookbook, *Oh Gussie! Cooking and Visiting in Kimberly's Southern Kitchen*.

Four-year-old Kimberly enjoys Christmas morning.

For more than sixty years, Christmas Eve has been spent at my grandmother's house. She's ninety-one years old and the tradition still goes on. The whole family gathers for an early supper while the kids rush us along because they can't stand to eat when they know we have presents waiting for them. After we open presents and play with the new toys, we visit and then it's off to my sister's house on Christmas Eve night. It's about bedtime when we arrive so my mother hands out wrapped identical packages to everybody—and we pretend like we don't know what's inside.

Opening these gifts, we find matching pajamas. Sometimes they are pretty, sometimes they are silly. Mom struggles to find matching pajamas for everyone in the family. In October, she starts freaking out about what is she going to do for pajamas. After everybody changes into their pajamas, we gather around my daddy as he reads the Christmas story out of the Bible. That is just becoming more and more special because I'm old enough to appreciate

> AFTER EVERYBODY CHANGES INTO THEIR **PAJAMAS,** *we gather around my daddy as he reads the* CHRISTMAS STORY OUT OF THE BIBLE.

the value of life. I don't know how much longer I'm going to have my daddy, so I cherish every time he sits in that rocking chair and reads the Christmas story.

After the reading, we put out cookies and milk for Santa by the Christmas tree and then scoot the kids off to bed. We sleep at my sister's house, which is crammed full with the kids sleeping on cots on the floor. Of course, they're all awake very early the next morning—but we don't let them come downstairs first. Another little tradition is to arrange the kids in order of their age on the staircase— the oldest sits on top and the youngest sits on the bottom. We've got pictures of that each year. Once that's done, we let them run in and see what Santa Claus brought them.

I would say I identify most with Mary in the Christmas story, not because she was chosen by God, but because she was a mom. We hear how glorious and perfect the birth of Jesus was. But when you stop and think about what happens in childbirth, when you think about the fact that a very, very pregnant woman was lying in hay or straw and nothing was

comfortable for her, I marvel at what she went through. And, as a mother, knowing there wasn't a soft place to put her baby or to make her baby comfortable, I can't imagine how she did it. I believe God used the animals and hopefully the innkeeper and his wife came to bring her cloth and water.

I think about Mary birthing her first child because I remember every detail of birthing my first and only child. And the fact that she rode on a donkey, I can't imagine what she went through. I'm not saying I feel like Mary, but I sure identify with her.

Kimberly SCHLAPMAN

FAVORITE CHRISTMAS RECIPE

MAMA'S TEA CAKES

INGREDIENTS
1 ¼ cups sugar
⅔ cup Crisco shortening
2 eggs
1 tablespoon milk; whole milk or half and half cream works best
1 teaspoon vanilla extract
3 cups flour, sifted
2 teaspoons baking powder
1 teaspoon salt

DIRECTIONS
Preheat oven to 375° F.
Tip: I use White Lily self-rising flour and leave off baking powder and salt.

Cream sugar, shortening, eggs, milk, vanilla. Combine flour, baking powder, and salt. Blend into egg mixture. Roll to ⅛-inch thick on lightly floured surface. Knead, roll out, cut with cookie cutter. I spray or lightly rub Crisco on baking sheet. Bake 8 to 10 minutes or until light brown.

Optional Icing: Combine 1 box powdered sugar and 1 stick softened butter; add touch of milk for proper consistency. Drizzle on top.

THEREFORE
the Lord himself
WILL GIVE YOU A SIGN:
THE VIRGIN WILL CONCEIVE AND GIVE BIRTH TO A SON,
AND WILL CALL HIM
Immanuel.

Isaiah 7:14

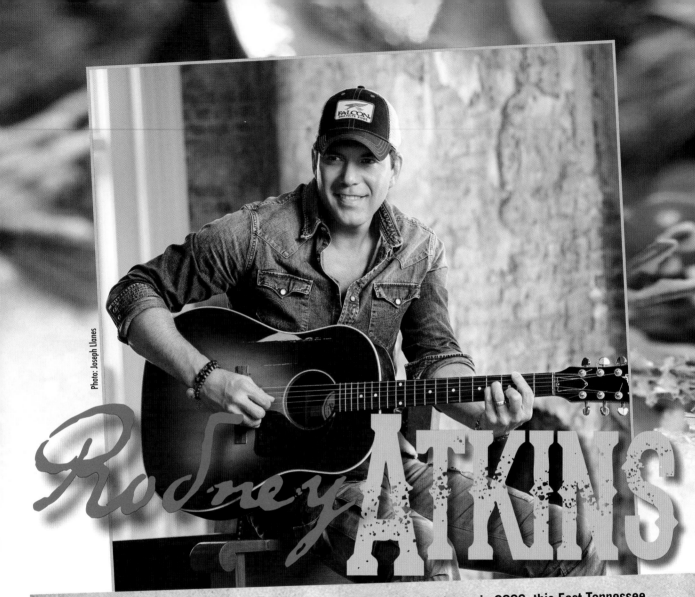

Photo: Joseph Llanes

Rodney ATKINS

Winner of the Academy of Country Music's Top New Male Vocalist honor in 2006, this East Tennessee native has thus far scored six No. 1 hits including "Take a Back Road," "If You're Going Through Hell (Before the Devil Even Knows)," and "Watching You," with the latter two songs each spending four weeks at the top of the charts, and earning Country Song of the Year in Billboard magazine's year end issues in 2006 and 2007.

We always get together with friends and family. Christmas Eve is spent with friends and family sharing food and gifts, and Christmas Day is with my parents and my sister. On the 24th, with the occasional exception of a newly discovered recipe unveiled, our menu pretty much is unchanged. It's ham, Mom's potato salad, meatballs, shrimp cocktail, and rolls. There's plenty of leftovers on Christmas Day, so nobody has to be cooking and no one is hungry.

Of course, as a kid the biggest event was Santa visiting on Christmas Eve. The first thing Christmas morning I couldn't wait to see what he left behind. I'll never forget getting my first 20-gauge shotgun one year. And in high school I got my first acoustic guitar—a black and red Dixon guitar. The first Christmas song I learned to play on it was "Away in a Manger." And through my childhood years there was always some live Nativity scene happening somewhere

> I THINK MOST FOLKS *with kids* WOULD AGREE THAT THE HOLIDAY, *recaptures its* *magic* WHEN YOU HAVE CHILDREN.

that we were a part of in the community. We would also go caroling with the folks my dad worked with from time to time, as well as attend Christmas Choir Cantatas that he directed.

These days, Christmas at our house is an especially cherished time of the year. It's when I'm usually off the road for a while and Elijah gets a break from school. I think most folks with kids would agree that the holiday recaptures its magic when you have children. Elijah just became a teenager. He's already thirteen and it seems that time is flying. That alone makes the season time-sensitive and special. Although he's not thinking about the fact that in a few short years he will probably be off to college, and ultimately raising a family of his own, I have.

We have held on to most of our traditions from my childhood with Elijah. Decorating the tree is a family event. We add a few new ornaments every year to mark special moments we were blessed with as the year comes to an end. We have added the "Elf on the Shelf" to our December tradition list. It's a lot of fun figuring out where the little guy shows up every morning after reporting in to Santa the night before. It's also a time of prayer and remembering the birth of our Lord. We attend church services, and have close family time talking and sharing stories about the true meaning of Christmas.

My beautiful Italian wife, Rose, loves to create in the kitchen. She always makes sure there is plenty of great food and GAMES! There is never a dull moment, and a lot of laughs fill our house during Christmas. And when I think about the Christmas story it's the shepherds that I identify with the most. They were not only the "common men," but also the ones who became outriders to spread the word of the Savior's birth. They even became a metaphor for Christ's love and the care He would provide for His flock. It's a reminder of what I am really to be about while on this earth, not just at Christmas, but every day—all year long.

Photo: Jennifer Rose

SNOWBALL CAKE

This is one of our very favorite cakes. We served it at our first "Married Christmas," with both of our families in attendance. My dad, "Papaw," liked it so much, he requested it for his birthday cake!

CAKE INGREDIENTS
1 box of your favorite chocolate cake mix
1 ½ cups milk
1 cup vegetable oil
1 3.4-ounce box instant vanilla pudding
3 eggs

DIRECTIONS
Beat cake ingredients on medium for 2 minutes or until well blended. Pour into 2 greased 9 inch, round cake pans.
Bake at 350° for 20–30 minutes or until you can poke it with a fork and the fork comes out clean; cool completely before frosting.

FROSTING INGREDIENTS
16-ounce container Cool Whip
6 chopped Hershey Bars
8 ounces softened cream cheese
½ cup powdered sugar
½ cup granulated sugar

DIRECTIONS
Place cream cheese and both sugars in a large bowl and beat with electric hand mixer until smooth. Add Cool Whip to bowl with sugar and cream cheese and blend until smooth. Gently fold chopped Hershey bars into whipped mixture. Frost layer one; place layer two on top of layer one and frost entire cake. Refrigerate and serve later—or serve right away!

Left: Rodney picnics with wife Rose.

Today in the town of David

A SAVIOR,

HAS BEEN BORN TO YOU;

HE IS THE

Messiah,

THE LORD.

Luke 2:11

THE SWON Brothers

Colton and Zach Swon.

Photo: Courtesy Alli

Oklahoma natives Zach and Colton Swon have been on stage since they were kids performing as part of their family's band. In 2013, they finished in third place on the fourth season of NBC's *The Voice*. Signing with Arista Nashville, they released their self-titled label debut in the fall of 2014 and scored their first hit with the single "Later On."

ZACH

Growing up, we never really did the "wake up Christmas morning and open your presents" thing. We just liked to sleep in. The cool thing that developed into a tradition was after we got home really late at night from visiting family on Christmas Eve, Mom cooked breakfast and we would do all our presents really, really early in the morning and stay up through the night just hanging out as a family.

COLTON

He's leaving out that every year our dad would act like he didn't want to stay up late. He'd say, "I'm too tired for it. I can't do it. Let's wait till the morning." We'd say, "Okay, we'll just go to bed." But then they'd come and knock on our doors and say, "Let's open the presents!" I think the reason we did it at night was because we are just musicians and we've always been night owls. Eating breakfast at two or three in the morning was awesome.

ZACH

Church was a part of our Christmas celebration. That's just what we believe in and how we were raised. We looked forward to it every year. There was always some kind of production at church. Our church wasn't huge so it wasn't like these mega productions with the baby in the manger, but it still was pretty cool though to go to church and get the Word.

COLTON

Back at home, we'd gather around the piano. My mom actually plays piano and sings with her brother. They have vinyl records that I still have just to make fun of the way they looked back then. I remember making the transition when we started playing instruments and playing piano, we would end up kicking our mom off and rocking out to some Bob Seger or something.

I grew up watching Garth Brooks and my dad play their black acoustic guitars so I just wanted my own black acoustic guitar. But the guitars were always so big and I was a little guy—still am. We finally found a black acoustic guitar that was a miniature version of my dad's. I could actually put my hands around it to start making the chords. I was probably seven at the time.

ZACH

My favorite gift was my drum set. When I was probably three or four years old, I wanted to play drums. My parents found this drum set that was a full drum kit, just a miniature version. It's really crazy that I still have this thing. It has a little drum and a cymbal coming out of it. That's what I learned how to play on. I started playing drums for my parents' gospel band when I was seven or eight years old.

COLTON

If I were living back during the first Christmas, I think I'd be more of a watcher—in awe of what's going on, or maybe one of the Wise Men bringing gifts. If I could get a chance to actually go see baby Jesus—and you know He's going to be the future king—I would be the one bringing gifts. I'd be like, "Oh my gosh, we gotta get in good with this guy."

ZACH

Colton is definitely a giver. He'd give somebody his last dollar. I am probably more selfish. I'm being honest. He amazes me sometimes the way he does that. If I had been living back then, I'd probably be the innkeeper because I'm the guy who it takes awhile for my conscience to kick in. I'd probably be the guy who said, "Oh, we don't have any room"—and then I'd feel really bad and give them what I had.

FAVORITE CHRISTMAS RECIPE

PARMESAN VEGETABLE TOSS

INGREDIENTS
2 cups mayonnaise or salad dressing
½ cup grated Parmesan cheese
¼ cup sugar
½ teaspoon dried basil
½ teaspoon salt
4 cups fresh broccoli florets
4 cups fresh cauliflower florets
1 medium red onion, sliced
1 8-ounce can sliced water chestnuts, drained
1 large head iceberg lettuce
1 pound sliced bacon, cooked and crumbled
2 cups croutons (optional)

DIRECTIONS
In large bowl, combine mayonnaise, Parmesan cheese, sugar, basil, and salt. Add broccoli, cauliflower, onion, and water chestnuts. Cover and refrigerate overnight. Just before serving, place lettuce in salad bowl and top with vegetable mixture. Sprinkle with bacon and croutons if desired.

Photo: Courtesy Dennis Carney

Know as Little Miss Dynamite, Brenda Lee's talent has spanned multiple genres and earned her inductions into the Country Music, Rock 'n Roll, and Rockabilly Halls of Fame. A recipient of the Grammy Lifetime Achievement Award, Lee has recorded forty-seven chart-topping hits, including "I'm Sorry" and "Rockin' Around the Christmas Tree"—a holiday classic for over fifty years.

Photo: Courtesy Brenda Lee

When I was growing up in rural Georgia, I was a poor daughter of the south, as most everybody else was. We didn't have all the gifts. We didn't have all the beautiful store-bought ornaments. What we had was a love of family and a belief in the love of God and that's what we had. Not to say that we didn't get gifts. My daddy was a great whittler and he made most of our toys.

The first store-bought doll I ever got at Christmas was when I was maybe ten or twelve years old. My daddy made our toys and we made our decorations. We would get things like evergreen branches or sticks or whatever we could find to make decorations. Sometimes we would cut out things from old magazines that someone had read and passed along to us. That's how we decorated our tree. We went out in the woods and cut our tree. Sometimes it would be a scrawny tree, and other times it would be a good-shaped one. But in our eyes, they were all beautiful.

MY DADDY MADE OUR TOYS, *and we made our decorations.*

The important thing to us was that everybody got together at Christmas. We always had food and lots of it on holidays. A lot of times back then, families lived with other families. There might be three families living in the same house. So there were a lot of us. We got hand-me-down toys. My first bicycle was a boys' bike I got when I was around seven years old. It was painted bright red and I thought it was the greatest thing that ever happened.

Church was always a big part of our Christmas celebration. During the year we went to church three times a week, like most people did where I lived. We always went to prayer meeting on Wednesdays and to church twice on Sunday. The church was our home away from home. That's where we went for our extracurricular activities, like picnics on the ground. And that's where we learned about God. No wonder at Christmas time I identify the most with the wise men—because they sought out Christ and found Him just as we did.

BRENDA LEE'S SQUASH CASSEROLE

INGREDIENTS
8 to 10 medium squash; washed with ends cut off.
  slice them up
1 large onion; sliced
1 can cream of mushroom soup
3 tablespoons sour cream
Cheddar Cheese grated
2 sleeves Ritz Crackers
1 stick butter
Salt and pepper to taste

DIRECTIONS
Add the onions to the sliced squash. Get the squash tender, then place in a colander and get as much liquid off of it as you can, even if you have to take paper towels and mash it down. Put that in a casserole dish. Mix up one can of cream of mushroom soup. On the sour cream, I mix it in to where it is not as much as the cream of mushroom, but 3 big tablespoons full. Stir that up and taste it and make sure that neither one overpowers the other. Into that, mix in grated cheddar, like sharp cheddar until it's mixed in and that's all pretty solid mixture. Then add two sleeves of Ritz crackers crumbled up. Heat or microwave a stick of butter and pour the Ritz crackers into the butter and get that all mixed in with the Ritz crackers. If you need more butter, add more. Dollop that out across the squash and make it smooth across the squash. Put the Ritz cracker mix over that mix. If you need more Ritz crackers and butter to cover it, just make what you need. All that needs to be covered. Put 3 or 4 slices of butter on top of that, and you can add more cheese on top depending on how much cheese you like. I usually put my cheese in it. It's better that way—to put your cheese in it, not on top. Put it on 350° F; let those crackers brown, because everything in it is already cooked. The cheese needs to melt inside it.

WHEN THEY *saw the* STAR, THEY WERE *overjoyed.*

Matthew 2:10

With more than twenty-five years in the country music industry, this two-time Grammy Award winning artist has sold nearly 60 million records and scored thirty-five No. 1 hits with fifty singles landing in the Top 10. He's won one hundred fifty music industry honors—including eighteen Academy of Country Music Awards and sixteen Country Music Association Awards.

Alan JACKSON

Below: Alan, wife Denise, and daughters Mattie, Dani, and Ali.

Photo: Courtesy Frederick Breedon IV

I just love Christmas. It's one of my favorite times of the year. I just can't wait to hear the Christmas songs on the radio or wherever and get the lights going and the decorations put up. I love thinking about the Christmas story. I admit I identify with the donkey because I'm stubborn and hardheaded. He played an important role carrying Mary to Bethlehem, so he was vital.

When I was growing up in Newnan, Georgia, we were pretty standard and simple on Christmas. One thing that I remember on Christmas morning was my parents never let us go into the living room where the tree and the presents were 'til everybody was up. You couldn't sneak in there. It seemed like my daddy moved as slow as he could to get ready, get up, and he had to drink his coffee. Everybody went crazy. Then we'd open presents and have a big Christmas lunch. We called it dinner then, but at lunchtime we had all the big stuff we have in the south—turkey, dressing, and standard vegetables and desserts.

When I was really young, my grandmother and granddaddy lived next

IT SEEMED MY DADDY MOVED AS *slow* AS HE COULD TO GET READY... *Everybody went* CRAZY.

door, and everybody lived nearby. We were kind of like the Waltons, all living right there. When all the grandchildren were really young we'd end up at my grandmother's— all the different families making an appearance. As they got older, everybody went their own way, but for a while that's how it was. As far as today, on Christmas Eve, we go to church. We've always done that. A lot of times we like to go ride around that same night and look at Christmas lights like we did when our three daughters were little; that's a lot of fun.

On Christmas morning, it's pretty much the same. We get up in the morning and have their Christmas, open gifts and stuff with our three daughters, and then we have a dinner. We have the same kinds of food that we did when we were young. We still call it the Christmas menu, things you have only once a year. We just hang around and do the regular stuff. We don't have a lot of immediate family, so we don't do that on Christmas day, but a lot of times we'd go back to Georgia.

When it comes to a favorite Christmas gift, as a child I don't remember getting anything that changed my life. I was just glad to get anything, as we didn't have much. Now that I'm older, nothing can ever beat Denise giving back my Thunderbird in 1993. I sold that car when we were first married and then years later, Denise tracked it down and bought it back for me. That was the sweetest gift anybody could give me—other than the babies.

Photo: Courtesy Alan Jackson

CHRISTMAS FRUIT SALAD

BOTTOM LAYER INGREDIENTS
1 6-ounce package lime gelatin
2 heaping cup vanilla ice cream
1 16-ounce can crushed pineapple, drained
DIRECTIONS Mix lime gelatin according to package directions using 1 cup boiling water and 1 cup cold water. Add ice cream and pineapple, stirring until ice cream is dissolved. Pour in large mold or 9 x 13 dish. Refrigerate until completely set.

MIDDLE LAYER INGREDIENTS
16 ounces sour cream
1 cup mayonnaise
2 cups chopped walnuts
DIRECTIONS
Mix sour cream, mayonnaise, and walnuts. Spread on lime mixture and return to refrigerator.

TOPPING INGREDIENTS
1 6-ounce package raspberry gelatin
1 16-ounce package frozen strawberries, sliced and thawed
2 ½ cups miniature marshmallows
DIRECTIONS Mix raspberry gelatin according to package directions using 1 ½ cups boiling water and 1 ½ cups cold water. Stir in strawberries and marshmallows. Allow to cool completely before adding to salad. Then gently pour over sour cream layer. Refrigerate overnight. Cut into squares or unmold and serve on iceberg lettuce.

Left: Alan visits with Santa Claus.

Dustin LYNCH

His first two albums were chart-toppers landing at No. 1 and No. 2 respectively thanks to platinum and gold singles "Cowboys and Angels" and "Where It's At." He's been nominated for two American Country Awards, and a CMT and ACM award for Top New Artist.

Above: Dustin and his sister Kristin Leigh Nichols share Santa's lap.
Left: Dustin prepares to indulge in Mom's Christmas cookies.

In my hometown, Tullahoma, Tennessee, we wait for two different things each year: the County Fair and the Christmas parade during the first or second week of December. The whole town shuts down when we have the Christmas parade. Different organizations like 4-H, the Shriners, the fire department, or any organization that wants to participate can enter a float and drive down the main drag. They throw out candy canes and all different kinds of treats. It's just a blast that kicks off the season for us and gets everybody fired up.

As far as my family goes, we do Christmas at our house and then we meet up at my aunt's house early afternoon. One tradition that my grandmother started a few years ago is a pickup basketball game. It's hilarious because she's eighty years old and she's right in the middle of the basketball court. She also plays piano at the church so we gather around the piano and do Christmas carols as a family. She makes up little programs like we're putting on a little church program for everybody.

The candlelight service at our church in Tullahoma grew into what is now the living nativity where they set up a live nativity scene in the lot across from the church with Bethlehem, candles, cows, and every character. It's a really cool annual reenactment. We'll go down there with the family each year and take that in, if I can get to town. For my nieces and nephews, it's really exciting because they've never seen cattle before and they don't have a clue what's going on. For a small town, it's a pretty incredible event that they put together.

Christmas has really transformed into a season of giving for me. Last year we started our first Christmas charity event called "Caring for Kids" in Tullahoma. They use what we raise to take a group of underprivileged kids shopping for coats and shoes and things that they can use for a while, not necessarily toys they'll play with for two days and then get tired of. I've been put into a position to where I can raise awareness for underprivileged people and it's fun to give back to a town that gave so much to me.

Speaking of gifts, when I was a kid my dad bought himself a guitar and me a miniature guitar. I think I was eight or ten years old. Naturally, I didn't want to play the one he got me—I wanted to play his! So this big old chunky Washburn guitar is the one I learned how to play on. He tried to play for a little bit but then just gave it up. I just kept on rocking with it. I started wanting to get better and sing when I was about fourteen.

That whole time of year is great. It used to be about opening presents, but now I've got a niece and nephew and I'm at a spot where I enjoy giving and watching people open their gifts and presents. As far as which character in the Christmas story I most identify with, being on the road with a bunch of wild animals and trying to keep the train on the track, I would go with shepherd.

MOM'S CHRISTMAS COOKIES

INGREDIENTS
3¾ cups sifted flour
1½ teaspoons baking powder
1 teaspoon salt
1 cup butter, softened
1½ cups sugar
2 teaspoons vanilla
2 eggs

DIRECTIONS
Preheat oven to 375° F. Sift flour with baking powder and salt and set aside. Cream butter, sugar, and vanilla until light and fluffy. Add eggs, 1 at a time, beating well after each egg. Slowly mix in dry ingredients until just blended (lowest speed if using a mixer).

If your kitchen is very hot, cover dough and chill about 1 hour. Roll out dough on a piece of foil the size of cookie sheet and cut out shapes using cookie cutters. Peel away extra dough from around shapes and put foil with cookies on cookie sheet. Bake 8–9 minutes until pale tan. Cool on wire racks.

INGREDIENTS
⅓ cup butter, softened
1 1-pound box confectioners sugar
5–6 tablespoons light cream (milk may be used)
2 teaspoons vanilla
¼ teaspoon salt

DIRECTIONS
Cream butter until fluffy; beat in sugar, a little at a time, adding alternately with cream. Mix in vanilla and salt and beat until satiny and of good spreading consistency. Stir in food coloring. Spread over warm cookies. Let dry overnight. Store in an airtight container with wax paper between layers of cookies.

Diamond RIO

Photo: Russ Harrington

For nearly three decades Marty Roe, Dan Truman, Dana Williams, Gene Johnson, Jimmy Olander, and Brian Prout have entertained audiences with an extensive arsenal of hits, charting more than thirty songs including such No. 1 hits as "Meet in the Middle," "One More Day," and "I Believe." They have won four Group of the Year honors from the Country Music Association and two Top Vocal Groups honors from the Academy of Country Music as well as a Gospel Music Association Dove Award and a Grammy.

Clockwise from left: Jim Olander, Dana Williams, Gene Johnson, Dan Truman, Brian Prout, and Marty Roe.

Marty ROE

(Diamond Rio)

Marty's first Christmas.

Photo: Modern Management

My dad was the youngest of four and mother was the oldest of nine living in Kentucky so we spent a lot of Christmases in eastern Kentucky. For the most part, Christmases were spent at one of my grandparents' houses with my cousins, a large group of people and a lot of good country cookin', and sharing music a lot. I'm fifty-four years old and I've never missed a Christmas with my parents.

On Christmas Eve, my kids and my brother's kids act out the Christmas story as we read from Luke. The kids play the roles and there's always a little squabble over who gets to be Mary and the Baby.

The character in the Christmas story I'm most curious about is Joseph's role. I've studied some in the last few years or so. It's pretty easy to gravitate towards Mary and the great faith that she had while basically being looked down upon as a woman with an illegitimate child.

But if you study why Mary and Joseph were in Bethlehem it was to be back in their hometown. I think about Joseph and how he showed up unmarried with a pregnant woman. I'm sure some family members shunned him. Just look at the treatment they got when they came to their hometown. The best someone could do was put them in a barn. The whole entrance of the Savior of the world was so counter-culture and counter to what we would perceive as an amazing event, came to the common man. Which is why the Christian side of Christmas is the main part of our lives. We worship the Christ and the greatest story ever told.

Gene JOHNSON

(Diamond Rio)

I grew up on a farm and was the youngest of three kids. We lived just outside of Sugar Grove, Pennsylvania. We averaged two hundred inches of snow a year—you can imagine winters were kind of tough, but it was a loving Christmas. We were not a well-to-do family. I got a lot of new clothes and things like that, nothing extremely memorable as a child.

My most memorable Christmas didn't come until I was twenty-three years old when I married my wife, June, at the First Presbyterian Church, Sugar Grove, PA, on Christmas Eve. We didn't take off anywhere on a honeymoon. We didn't have the money. I remember fixing a nice fire in the fireplace and putting a mattress down on the floor where we spent our first night. That was 1972, so it will be coming up on forty-three years.

Gene placing the ornament his sister Hazel made fifty-five years ago.

Dana WILLIAMS

(Diamond Rio)

....

I love the attitude change that you feel and see in people at Christmas. It just warms your heart and it also raises the question,

WHY CAN'T WE BE LIKE THAT ALL YEAR?

The main thing about Christmas for me is the reminder of the birth of Christ and what Jesus has meant to us our whole life. That first Christmas I would have been one of the townspeople standing there in awe with my mouth open. I just think the reality of what was actually happening there is so beyond our comprehension. It's not just the birth of a child, but the birth of our Savior.

FAVORITE CHRISTMAS RECIPE

SWEDISH KORV Gene Johnson Recipe

We may change up what we have for dinner from year to year, but our Christmas breakfast is always the same and that's KORV, a Swedish word for "potato sausage," and it is especially delicious when served with pancakes or French toast with pure maple syrup. We use allspice—that's what makes this sausage distinctive. If you can't taste the allspice, it isn't KORV!

INGREDIENTS
2 pounds venison, ground once. Or substitute lean beef.
1 pound lean pork, ground once
2 medium onions, very finely chopped
1 pound potatoes, boiled but still solid
1 tablespoon salt   1 tablespoon pepper
1 tablespoon Allspice   1 cup milk

DIRECTIONS
Do not overcook potatoes or they will be too mushy. Run potatoes through a food chopper to a "fine" chop. TIP: if you cook the potatoes the night before and let them chill, it is easier to process. Using your hands, blend all ingredients thoroughly; wear gloves. Use natural casings that have been thoroughly cleaned and all salt removed. Run the mixture through the chopper without the blades and, using a spout, fill casings. Tie off casings in about twelve-inch lengths. Leave room in filled casing for expansion. Simmer in water for 30–45 minutes; to eliminate air bubbles prick sausage before water boils. Alternative method: If you don't like natural casings, form mixture into patties and cook on very low heat until tender.

Above, left: Dana's First Christmas in new home with family (son, stepdaughter, Dana and wife, mom, sister, dad). Above, right: Young Dana and sister Scarlett in Christmas wagon.

jamie O'NEAL

Born in Sydney, Australia, Jamie O'Neal honed her skills as a background vocalist with international pop star Kylie Minogue before settling in Nashville and launching a successful career as a country artist. Her first studio album, *Shiver*, spawned two back to back No. 1 hits, "There Is No Arizona" and "When I Think About Angels." These days, in addition to recording and touring, O'Neal produces at her recording studio and operates her own record company, Momentum Label Group.

We were on the road so much back when I was a child, that every Christmas was a little different each year. When it came to hiding the presents from us until Christmas, my parents had to be pretty creative since we mostly lived out of an RV. The fact that our RV didn't have an "official" chimney meant that Santa had his work cut out delivering the gifts. Now with my own family, even though we are often traveling, church is part of our Christmas celebration. We usually sing hymns for the congregation every year in Gray, Tennessee, when we go to visit my husband's family.

When I think of the most special Christmas it has to be in 2013. My sweet mother-in-law Sandra Ford had cancer and, as it turned out, that was her last Christmas with us. Even though she was weak she managed to lead the choir at Gray Methodist Church which made everything extra special. The angels took her home in July 2014, and Christmas, our favorite time of the year, was very different for us that year. We will always light a candle for her and sing in church in her honor.

My husband, Rod, our daughter, Aliyah, and I love to celebrate Christmas—and even our pets get in on the celebration. For me Christmas with our pups is really important. Griffin, my sixteen-year-old Maltese passed over the "rainbow bridge" last summer, but I set out photos of him ripping into his gifts which has been a big part of our Christmas fun.

Photos: Courtesy Jamie O'Neal

Top: Jamie with husband Rod and daughter Aliyah. Below: Chelsea unwraps the gifts.

From that very first night when Jesus made His entrance in the manger in Bethlehem and the wise men came bearing gold, frankincense, and myrrh, gifts have always been a part of the Christmas celebration.

I'm blessed with a wonderful husband, and when I think back on presents I've received, the most memorable is a very special painting from Rod—it's a pretty little white kitten sitting in a big purple chair, very eclectic and colorful. He knew how much I loved it so he surprised me with it.

Surprising people with gifts is something I truly love doing. When I think about the people in the Christmas story whom I most identify with, it's probably the wise men because they bring gifts and I love gift giving! It's such a happy thing to pick out gifts and wait for your loved ones' response.

Australian Roast Potatoes

INGREDIENTS
Golden potatoes, enough for two per person
2 cups flour
Cayenne red pepper
Garlic salt
Onion powder
Salt and pepper
Olive oil

DIRECTIONS
This recipe is all about spicing the potatoes to taste, so there's no measuring of the spices. Start by peeling and cutting potatoes into four pieces. Rinse. Roll slightly damp potatoes into a mix of flour, cayenne red pepper, garlic salt, onion powder, salt, and pepper. Heat 1/2 inch of olive oil in a roasting pan prior to putting potatoes in the oil. After putting potatoes in the oil—or, if you've made a roast turkey, roast beef, or roast chicken you may put oil in bottom of pan and put potatoes around the meat—sprinkle with rosemary (optional) and cook at 400° F for 20 minutes. Turn potatoes over at midpoint and cook another 25 minutes or until crispy on outside, soft on inside. Yum!!

They saw the child with his
MOTHER MARY,
AND THEY BOWED DOWN
AND WORSHIPED HIM.
THEN THEY OPENED THEIR
TREASURES AND PRESENTED
HIM WITH GIFTS OF
gold, frankincense & myrrh.

Matthew 2:11

Marty
RAYBON

As lead singer for the Grammy winning band Shenandoah, Marty Raybon placed twenty-six songs on the country charts, including the No. 1 hits "The Church on Cumberland Road," "Sunday in the South," and "Two Dozen Roses." In addition to winning CMA and ACM awards with Shenandoah, Raybon has had a successful solo career in both the bluegrass and gospel fields.

....

When I was young, we literally were so poor that we spelled "poooor" with four zeros and that's just the truth. I don't regret any of that. In fact, I believe wholeheartedly that it made me who I am today. The value of things means something to me because I know what it takes to try to give to your kids when you don't have it to give. Even though Mother and

Photo: Courtesy Rural Rhythm Records

Daddy didn't have much, it was amazing how they could make up for it in other ways—like the way my mother decorated the house. Since she was good with her hands, making drapes and upholstery work and such, she'd hand make the centerpieces and decorations for our Christmas.

We didn't just celebrate Christmas because it was the time of year to give gifts to people. My Mama and Daddy both knew Christmas was a celebration of Who Christ was and what Christ had done. I understood all that. There was such joy in our house that time of year—the whole house radiated with the energy that my mother had which produced so much excitement for all of us. The last thing that my mother bought me was three pairs of argyle socks. I still have them.

What I have held onto since childhood is the reason for Christmas. We were taught to never forget that. I was gloriously saved in March of 1991. After salvation, that first Christmas meant more to me than any of the rest in my lifetime. Now, every year I celebrate Christmas with my wife and three sons by reading Luke 2 on Christmas Eve. We talk about the birth of Christ and we follow that with a

Left photo, from left to right: Michael, Matthew, Mary holding Jameson, Micah and Max. Right photo, from left to right: Melanie, Maxwell, Michael, Matthew, and Marty.

discussion of how we have seen the Lord move in our own lives throughout the year. We realize that we have been given the greatest gift that has ever been given!

Now that we have two grandsons, they're included in that family tradition. We talk about the Christmas story just like we did when their daddy was little. Sometimes, they'll say, "We've heard this. Daddy read it to us in the Bible before we came." And I'll say, "That's because your daddy knew we were going to do it again when you got here." Reading Luke 2 is an important part of our celebration and church is also an important part of our Christmas time. We usually have a Christmas program of some kind celebrating Him with a play or musical cantata.

Of course, gifts are part of the Christmas season. The best gift I ever got came from my wife, Melanie— a Study Bible back in the Christmas of 1991. I had been reading a lot of the Bible and it allowed me to understand the Word with insight and background to the scriptures. Although it's a little ragged, I still use it. When I'm reading about the Christmas story, the character I identify with the most would have to be the innkeeper. For so many years I never understood the importance of Who Christ was and what He wanted to be in me. I knew Him, but I had never made room in my heart.

I thank the Lord that He never stopped knocking.

FAVORITE CHRISTMAS RECIPE

CHRISTMAS TURKEY

INGREDIENTS
18-pound turkey
3 loaves of bread
2 large onions, chopped
3 green bell peppers, chopped
3 sticks of celery, chopped
1 tablespoon chopped garlic
1 ½ sticks of Land O'Lakes sweet cream butter, melted
1 tablespoon poultry seasoning
1 tablespoon sage
Salt and pepper to taste.

DIRECTIONS
Open the wrappers on the loaves of bread on both ends to let the bread air dry out for three or four days prior to preparing the stuffing. Then, tear bread into small pieces in a large mixing bowl. Add chopped onions, bell peppers, celery, and garlic, along with the poultry season, sage, salt and pepper to taste. Pour melted butter over the mixture and hand mix thoroughly. Wash the turkey by running cold water over it; remove neck and bagged goods out of the inner bird. Stuff the turkey with small handfuls of the stuffing in the inner part of the bird until filled. Do the same thing in the opening where the neck should be. Tie the legs together and place in a covered baking pan. Place in a preheated 500° F oven for one hour. Reduce the temperature to 325° and cook 20 minutes per pound. Let the turkey sit for cooling before carving.

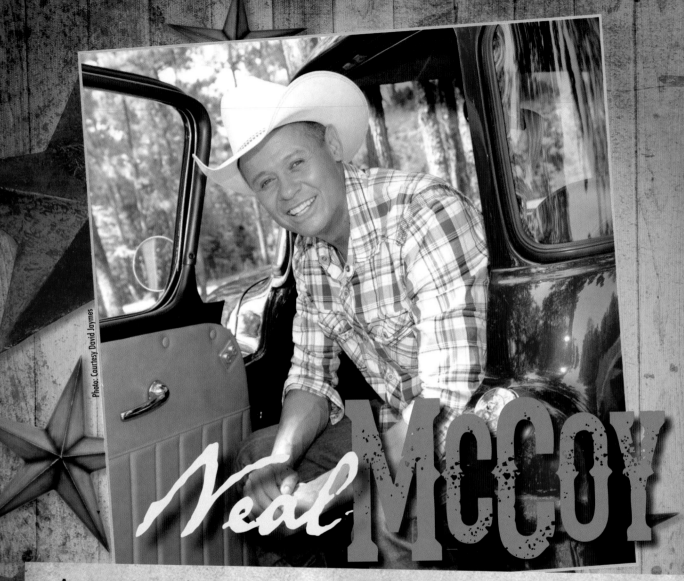

Photo: Courtesy David Jaymes

A consummate entertainer well known for his high-energy stage show, Neal McCoy has released ten albums and more than thirty-four singles, including the No. 1 singles "No Doubt About It" and "Wink." He's scored three platinum albums and one gold album certification. A two-time winner of the TNN/Music City News Entertainer of the Year Award, McCoy is a noted philanthropist who was honored with the Academy of Country Music/Home Depot Humanitarian Award in 2005.

Photo: Courtesy Neal McCoy

Growing up in Jacksonville, Texas, I had a brother four years older, and a sister three years older. I was the baby. Like typical kids we'd pester our mom and dad as early as we could on Christmas morning so we could get them out to the tree. We didn't have far to go with a little ole bitty house, but we wanted to wake them up so we could get out there and get our stuff. Unlike today, back then it was all about playing outside and whether it was a bicycle, a frisbee, a ball and glove, we wanted to get outside and start playing with whatever we had.

Neal with wife Melinda, daughter Miki, and son Swayde.

The funniest gift we ever got was one of those sand bag things that you blow up and you hit them and they fall over and pop back up. You punch the nose and it makes noise. I forget what this one was designed as—maybe a clown. When my brother and I were maybe five and nine or something, we slipped out of our rooms in the dark and we could just see the shadow of that thing. We were scared but we sneaked up on it. We kind of pushed on it and he went down a little bit and came back.

Then my brother took a swing and hit him in the nose—the thing made a squeak which really scared us. We didn't have a lot growing up so we were just pretty excited about anything that we got. Neither of our parents were making a lot of money, but whatever they gave us we were pretty happy with it. The coolest gift I ever got was a Stingray bicycle with a banana seat!

On Christmas we'd go to my paternal grandmother and grandfather's house. They were right there in town. But my mother's side were mostly Filipinos, so we didn't see them because we didn't have anybody that lived around us. Once I had my own family, my wife, Melinda, and I started our own traditions. On Christmas Eve, we go to Melinda's mother and dad's house. Her dad passed away quite a few years ago, but we still go to her mother's house and somebody reads the Christmas story.

Then we have eggnog. Some choose with hooch and some without hooch. And I'm not too much of a hooch guy so I usually just get straight old eggnog. We'll do that Christmas Eve, and Christmas morning we wake up at our house and let our kids open presents. Our daughter has kids now. We open presents on Christmas morning and that night, my whole family comes up from Tyler and Jacksonville, Texas, and spends Christmas Day night with us at our house. We've been doing that for quite a few years. These days the kids are too old to leave Santa a note and cookies, but grandkids are falling in. So it will be fun to start doing that tradition of leaving cookies and the letter to Santa out for Santa to get. My daughter has two children and there's nothing like having grandkids!

My brother is the music director of the church I grew up in in Jacksonville, Texas. They have a candlelight service and we try to get down there when we can. We're pretty fortunate that we get to see most of our family around Christmastime. I feel sorry for a lot of folks who live across the country from each other and very seldom get to see each other.

PANCIT

Growing up with a Filipino mother, she cooked a lot of great dishes from the Philippines. They've got a great light noodle Filipino dish called Pancit. That's very non-traditional for you white folks. We also had Lumpia, which is a Filipino egg roll. As crazy as it is for a Christmas meal, it would have to be Pancit.

Photo: Courtesy Neal McCoy

INGREDIENTS

1 package rice noodles
2 cubes beef bullion
1 pound pork
Cooking oil
Minced garlic
Soy sauce
1 bag shredded carrots
1 small head cabbage chopped
1 bunch celery chopped

DIRECTIONS

Soak rice noodles in warm water. Cook two cubes of beef bullion according to instructions to make beef broth. I think it's 1 cube for 1 cup of water. Cut up pork in small pieces and brown it in wok or large pot with a little oil, a couple tablespoons of minced garlic, and a little soy sauce. Add chopped vegetables. Add in a little beef broth to help soften veggies. Let that cook until tender. Make sure noodles are softened, cut them with scissors into smaller sections. Makes it easier to mix and eat. Add noodles and mix well. Add the rest of beef broth. Just make sure you don't use too much broth. It will be too juicy. Add soy sauce...this is just by preference of how much you want. Mix and let it cook until everything is tender and blended together well.

AND THE CHILD
grew and became
STRONG;
HE WAS FILLED WITH
Wisdom,
AND THE GRACE OF GOD
WAS ON HIM.

Luke 2:40

Lee GREENWOOD

During his award winning career, Lee Greenwood has released twenty-two studio albums and seven compilation albums, delivering seven No. 1 hit singles including "Dixie Road," and "Hearts Aren't Made to Break (They're Made to Love)." The Grammy winning singer/songwriter/author is best know for his patriotic anthem "God Bless the USA." Greenwood has received the Congressional Medal of Honor Society's National Patriots Award and entertained troops on more than thirty USO Tours.

....

When I moved to Tennessee I married into a great family. At Christmas, my wife Kim and I always get the family together and have tacos. Now, I know that's kind of odd. But rather than turkey or ham, tacos are something I brought back from California. We grind our own taco shells—which my father-in-law taught us how to do with a taco press. In addition to that Christmas

tradition, we get a bunch of singers together and enjoy going to neighbors' houses caroling with little gas lanterns. We choose different neighborhoods in the Nashville area.

Kim is a very good cook. At Christmas she always makes pumpkin pies for us and she'll make another dozen pies for us to deliver to our friends and neighbors. Church is also part of our holidays When I'm not working, we'll slip into our church and attend the candlelight service on Christmas Eve.

My favorite memory is when I was eight or nine and I got my first BB gun—a Red Ryder with a lever action. You had to be careful—and it's funny because every person I eve talked to that got a BB gun when they were a small kid opened the lever and pulled the trigger and it would snap down and nearly break your finger. But the reason I was given a BB gun on the farm was because we had lots of trees with food around us. When I'd come home from school I was allowed to go out in the front yard and shoot the

Photo: Courtesy Lee Greenwood

Above: Lee with sons Parker and Dalton.

sparrows out of our fig tree because they would be eating our figs and we couldn't get the figs.

I had this long pole with a can on it with a sharp edge and we would get the figs at the very top of the tree that were the largest and bring them down, and of course make a basket so we'd have figs to eat that night or the next day. I had a little hunter cat that would walk with me, named Marmalade, and when I'd shoot the bird she would grab the bird and take it to her kittens. But that's a great memory, receiving my first BB gun at Christmas.

I love the Christmas season and every year I have to relearn the Christmas songs because naturally we don't do them for a whole year, and it's so fun to have a first rehearsal and go through that, relearning the songs, redoing them with my band, and bringing up the tracks, and getting prepared for our first Christmas show, getting the sets out so we can travel with those. It's just a wonderful joyous time and being able to go through the giving process where we give gifts to people.

I kind of identify with Joseph. We've had children and I know how it feels to escort your wife who's about to give birth to a beautiful miracle. Of course there's only one Christ, but when we had our children, I was by my wife's side every moment the last two or three weeks and watched her go through that transition. So, I identify with Joseph as the husband and the father.

Photo: Courtesy Lee Greenwood

Lee with sons Parker and Dalton, and wife Kimberly.

FAVORITE CHRISTMAS RECIPE

SWEET POTATO CASSEROLE

INGREDIENTS
1 large can sweet potatoes
1 stick of butter, melted
½ cup sugar
½ teaspoon ground cinnamon
2 eggs
¾ cup milk

DIRECTIONS
Drain can of potatoes and heat with butter.
Cream the potatoes along with remaining ingredients.
Bake uncovered at 400° F for 30 minutes.

TOPPING INGREDIENTS
1 cup crushed frosted flakes
½ cup brown sugar
1 cup broken pecans
½ stick of butter, melted

DIRECTIONS
Mix all ingredients, pour over potatoes.
Bake uncovered at 400° F for 5–7 minutes.

A member of both the Songwriters and Country Music Halls of Fame, this East Tennessee native has become a beloved entertainment icon with a successful career in TV, film, and music. She was won seven Grammy Awards, seven Academy of Country Music honors, and nine CMA Awards, including Entertainer of the Year.

"I like to say that I cook like an old mountain woman. Well, only a real mountain woman could spend all day smokin' the daylights out of a turkey."

Photo: Courtesy CTK Mgmt/Dolly Records

FAVORITE CHRISTMAS RECIPE

DOLLY PARTON'S SMOKY MTN SMOKED TURKEY BREAST

INGREDIENTS
4 or 5 tennis ball-sized hickory wood chunks
2 tablespoons coarsely ground pepper
1 6-pound) bone-in whole turkey breast, fresh or frozen, thawed
2 7-ounce bottles sweet chili pepper sauce

DIRECTIONS
If you use fresh turkey breasts, expect to cook them up to 6 hours. Soak the wood chunks in water for at least 1 hour. Prepare the charcoal fire in the smoker and let burn 30 minutes. Meanwhile, rub the pepper evenly over the turkey breast. Pour the pepper sauce all over the turkey breast to coat completely. Drain the wood chunks and place them directly on the coals. Place a water pan in the smoker and add water to the depth of the fill line. Place the turkey breast on the smoker rack and close the cover. Smoke the breast for 6 hours or until an instant-read thermometer inserted in the thickest part of the breast registers 170° F. If necessary, add water to the pan to maintain the level at the depth of the fill line. Transfer the turkey breast from the smoker to a cutting board and let stand 10 minutes before slicing.

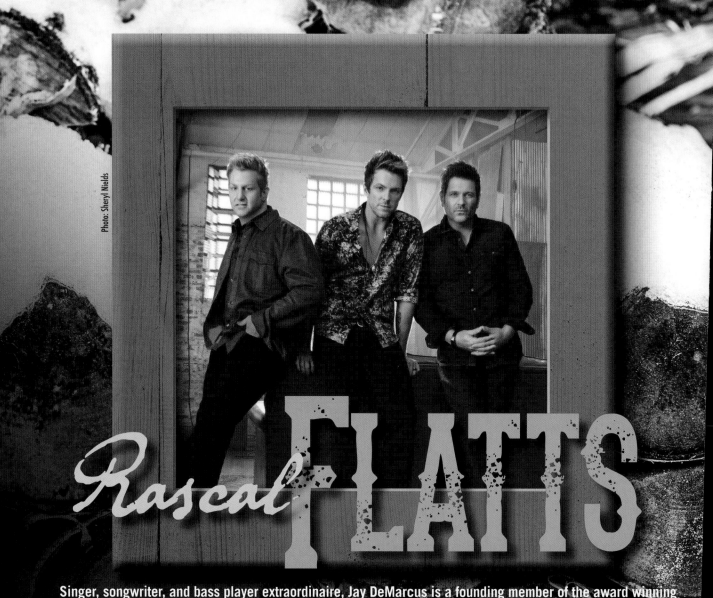

Photo: Sheryl Nields

Rascal FLATTS

Singer, songwriter, and bass player extraordinaire, Jay DeMarcus is a founding member of the award winning trio Rascal Flatts. Since debuting in 2000, DeMarcus, Gary LeVox, and Joe Don Rooney have sold nearly 23 million albums, over 29 million digital downloads, earned more than forty major industry awards, and have scored fifteen No. 1 hits, including "What Hurts the Most," "Fast Cars and Freedom," and "Bless the Broken Road." Eight consecutive albums (out of nine) debuted at No. 1 on Billboard's Top Country Albums chart.

Above, left to right: Gary LeVox, Joe Don Rooney, and Jay DeMarcus

Jay DeMARCUS

(Rascal Flatts)

When I was a child, the thing I remember most about Christmas is how we were always together. On Christmas Eve we would go to my grandparents' house where my sister and I could open up just one gift. It felt like every year we'd have to beg Mom and Dad to open that one gift. I think they loved that part of our tradition as much as we looked forward to it. They would drag out their decision. They'd say, "We'll see if you can open one—but we don't know yet if we'll let you." But of course, they did.

On Christmas Eve, we would also pile into one car and drive to downtown Columbus, Ohio, to see this huge nativity scene outside of one of the office buildings. The figures from the Christmas story were bigger than life—the wise men, the shepherds, all of the animals. It was a couple of stories high. We'd look at that nativity and then drive around downtown enjoying the lights. Columbus always had a lot of great holiday lights downtown. We did that every year growing up. My sister and I would make a pact: whoever woke up first on Christmas morning would wake up the other

> WHEN I THINK OF *the* CHRISTMAS STORY I MOST IDENTIFY WITH JOSEPH BECAUSE HE HAD TO FEEL REALLY OVERWHELMED BY EVERYTHING.

person. Sometimes we were trying to get up at 3 or 4 a.m. to see what Santa brought. I've carried a lot of those traditions on with my kids. We try to carry on some other traditions, too, like letting them go see Santa. We go to Cheekwood Botanical Garden and Museum of Art in Nashville and do pictures with Santa.

When I think back on Christmas gifts, the one I remember most is a set of maroon, late 1960s Gretsch drums. They were the greatest thing in the world! I loved those drums so much because they were my first real instrument. I'd had a lot of toys up to that point. But once my mom and dad saw I had serious interest in learning how to play music—and, at that point in time, the drums—they scraped together every dime they could and bought me that wooden Gretsch drum kit. Unfortunately, while we were on vacation one year, our basement flooded, the wood warped, and they were ruined. When I think of the Christmas story, I most identify with Joseph because he had to feel really overwhelmed by everything. He had to wonder why God would pick him for such a huge responsibility,

Photo: Sheryl Nields

Left to right: Gary LeVox, Joe Don Rooney, and Jay DeMarcus.

and why God chose to bless him as much as he was blessed. I'm sure he walked around in wonderment and amazement the whole time, hardly being able to believe he had been chosen to live such a life.

I'm eternally grateful that, when I was growing up, my parents never let us forget the reason we celebrate christmas.

In spite of the Christmas trees, the elves, Santa, and the gifts, they instilled in me that the real reason we celebrated was because the Savior was born and He was sent to earth to die in our place. I'm so grateful I had parents that cared enough to make sure we always remembered that Gift.

Rascal FLATTS

FAVORITE CHRISTMAS RECIPE

PUMPKIN ROLL   Jay DeMarcus Recipe

INGREDIENTS
3 eggs
1 cup white sugar
⅔ cup pumpkin
1 teaspoon lemon juice
¾ cup all purpose flour
1 teaspoon baking powder
2 teaspoons cinnamon
1 teaspoon ginger
½ teaspoon nutmeg
½ teaspoon salt

DIRECTIONS
Preheat oven to 375° F. Beat eggs on high speed in mixer for 5 minutes. Gradually beat in white sugar. Stir in 2/3 cup of pumpkin and 1 teaspoon of lemon juice. In a separate bowl stir together flour, baking powder, cinnamon, ginger, nutmeg, and salt. Fold into pumpkin mixture. Spread into greased and floured pan (15 x 10 x 1 inches). Bake at 375° F for 15 minutes. Turn out on towel sprinkled with confectioners sugar. Immediately roll up the cake, let it cool completely, then unroll and spread the filling.

Filling mixture:
1 cup confectioners powdered sugar
8 ounces Philadelphia cream cheese
4 tablespoons margarine
½ teaspoon vanilla
Combine powdered sugar, cream cheese, margarine, and vanilla; beat until smooth. Spread over cake and then roll it back up. Chill in the fridge or eat it. I also sprinkle confectioners sugar over the pumpkin roll because it just looks pretty!

For to us a child is born,
TO US A SON IS GIVEN,
AND THE GOVERNMENT WILL BE ON,
HIS SHOULDERS.
AND HE WILL BE CALLED
Wonderful Counselor,
Mighty God,
PRINCE OF PEACE.

Isaiah 9:6

Photo: Roy Burmiston

Hunter **HAYES**

His debut album went No. 1 on the Billboard Top Country Albums and was certified platinum; "Wanted" was a multi-platinum single with 3.5 million sold. Nominated for four Grammy Awards, he won the Country Music Association Award for New Artist of the Year in 2012.

My parents have always placed a lot of importance on dinner together every night. It wasn't about dinner; it was about time together to talk about our day or whatever. Family dinners were especially memorable at Christmas. We all lived within two hours of each other in Louisiana. For lunch, we would go to my mom's parents' house. The whole family would be there. Then we'd go to my dad's mom's house. We'd do the same kind of thing—just chill out and spend time together.

Church was also a big part of our celebration. The service was really musical. We didn't usually have a choir at our church, but we had one for Christmas. A couple of musicians would show up for the Christmas service. They planned it for weeks in advance so it was musically stunning. There were a ton of decorations, too. The whole church was just transformed. I'd never seen it look so good.

Typically we'd open gifts the first thing Christmas morning before church. One Christmas when I was twelve years old, I was an altar boy. That was the year I got my favorite Christmas present of all time—a Tascam 8-track recorder with a hard drive which meant you could edit things with it. I felt so bad because getting home and making music on that Tascam was the only thing I could think about during the service. I

Photo: Courtesy Hunter Hayes

wanted to make demos of my own for so long and I never really had the gear to do it.

That was the year I finished a Christmas album. I remember going back to the studio where I had recorded the Christmas album with the engineer—who ended up engineering my first two records here in Nashville. I would go back to the studio in Louisiana and ask him to help me figure out how to work that Tascam machine.

I was always involved with music, especially Christmas music. The band and I would do Christmas shows, starting when I was seven or eight. We played at corporate functions or Christmas festivals, church festivals, things like that. During those days, I was dreaming of a career in music. Getting that Tascam recorder was so important. Being in the studio and creating was an obsession.

Recording is one of my favorite parts of what I get to do. It's second only to actually getting on stage. The process of creating, writing, and demoing and all that stuff is such a cool process. I was obsessed with the concept that you could go into the studio with nothing and come out with something. And the fact that I now had a studio in my bedroom was a pretty big deal. I didn't come out of my room for like a year after that. You never saw me. That Christmas gift changed my life for sure.

I have to say the innkeeper is the character in the Christmas story I identify with the most because there are a lot of different interpretations of that particular character. When I was young, somebody gave a sermon where they said everybody assumes the innkeeper was mean when he told Mary and Joseph, "There's no room here." There's also the possibility he just literally didn't have any choice and he was just trying to figure it out. I don't know. If anything, I wish music was one of those gifts that the wise men would have brought. I wish I could have gone with a guitar and a couple of friends and sang to baby Jesus.

HOLIDAY COOKIE CUPS

INGREDIENTS
1 package sugar cookie dough
12 mini pretzels
2 tablespoons hot cocoa mix
½ cup heavy whipping cream
1 cup semi-sweet chocolate chips
½ cup white chocolate chips
1 cup mini marshmallows
Granulated white sugar

DIRECTIONS
Preheat oven to 375° F; grease 24 mini-muffin tins. Take 1 tablespoon of the sugar cookie dough and form into individual balls; roll each in sugar then press into and line the sides of the greased mini-muffin tins. Bake 12 to 14 minutes; cool cookies completely in the pan before carefully removing them.

To make the chocolate ganache: Bring whipping cream to a boil, stir in hot cocoa mix; pour the hot cocoa and cream over the semi-sweet chocolate chips. Allow this to sit for 3 minute before gently stirring until the chocolate chips are completely melted and the ganache is silky smooth. Snap off the loops of the mini pretzels to use as handles. Attach these handles to the cookie cups with melted white chocolate; Spoon the ganache into the cookie cups and top with mini marshmallows. It's best to store the Holiday Cookie Cups in the refrigerator.

AND SHE GAVE BIRTH TO HER FIRSTBORN,
A SON,
She wrapped him in cloths and placed him in a manger, BECAUSE THERE WAS
NO GUEST ROOM AVAILABLE FOR THEM.

Luke 2:7

This Georgia born and bred native got his start singing in church. He paid his dues pouring concrete and doing a stint as a personal trainer, while playing the club circuit at night. The Grammy-nominated artist has six albums and seventeen hit singles—including ten No. 1 songs.

As a kid, our Christmas mornings were really simple. Of course they started with my mom at our house waking us up. My brother, my sister, and myself—we were always up later than she was on Christmas Eve, looking to see what Santa Claus brought us. Of course we'd fall asleep, but when Mom woke us up Christmas morning, we'd go in there, open all the gifts that she and Santa would give. When we were done with that, we would have some breakfast and then go play outside with whatever we got. Around 1:00 p.m. we would always go to

Billy **CURRINGTON**

my grandma's house and have another Christmas. She would be the one that would cook the big meal. The majority of our Christmas was spent back at my grandma's house.

She cooked everything, really. If you name it, I guarantee you it was on that table. From turkey and ham, to homemade macaroni and cheese. My granddad and myself were big gardeners. We grew a lot of stuff like turnip greens, spinach, corn, tomatoes, and so a lot of the stuff we would be eating would be stuff that we had either canned in the fall or frozen.

People would talk about how great the food was that we grew ourselves. We were big fans of that, and I still am. I do a lot of that gardening—from sugar cane to seed corn. Right now I've got tomatoes and bok choy. I've got a list a mile long out there in the garden that I'm growing right now. When I was a kid, we would eat what we could eat fresh. What was left over that we didn't give away, we would just can.

During the holidays, there were church Christmas plays that we were in. I was always in the Christmas play. Since my grandma had me in the kids' choirs, I would always get picked for a part. They'd give me and the other kids a script to read, and we had to memorize our parts, and act them out—just like you

For me, because I'm a sailor, the people in the Christmas story I identify the most with are the wise men, the ones who were following the star to get to Jesus. I do a lot of traveling on the ocean at night time and I use the stars to get to where I'm going a lot. That's why I relate to those guys most, getting somewhere by following a star.

FAVORITE CHRISTMAS RECIPE

SKILLET MACARONI & CHEESE

A treasured recipe from South Georgia

INGREDIENTS
1½ cups sharp cheese, grated
1 cup macaroni, cooked and well-drained
½ cup sour cream
2 tablespoons butter
3 eggs, slightly whipped
2 cups milk
Salt and pepper to taste

DIRECTIONS
Mix cooked macaroni and cheese (grated on coarse side of the grater). Add eggs, sour cream, and salt and pepper to taste. Place in greased black skillet and top with ½ cup of sharp grated cheese. Bake 20 minutes in a 350° F oven. Don't worry if it shakes a little on the top, it will thicken up after being removed from the oven.

Luke
BRYAN

LUKE BRYAN'S
SCRAMBLED CHILI DOGS

One of my favorite holiday memories has turned into a holiday tradition. On Christmas Eve when we would have so many people over to visit, my mom started making chili dogs—we named them "Scrambled Dogs" because we layered them with toppings. They were such a hit with the family we did it year after year. Once the yearly tradition began, my mom enlisted my help and put me in charge of toasting the buns . . . and cutting the onions!

INGREDIENTS
1 pound ground beef
1 can tomato soup
1 small onion finely chopped
1–2 teaspoons chili powder
2 teaspoons mustard
Dash of olive oil

DIRECTIONS
Sauté chopped onion in dash of olive oil with ground beef. Stir in chili powder and mustard spice then add tomato soup. Simmer and serve. Add cheese, oyster crackers, and onions to taste on top. Serve with Luke's favorite Lay's potato chips on the side.

This Leesburg, Georgia, native is the reigning CMA and ACM Entertainer of the Year. Country music's most consistent hit-maker, Bryan's last three albums have debuted at No. 1 on Billboard's all genre Top 200 chart. His 2013 album, *Crash My Party*, spawned six consecutive No. 1 singles, including "That's My Kind of Night" and "Play It Again." His fifth album, *Kill the Lights*, released in August 2015 and sold more than 320,000 copies the first week.

The 1st Sunday of ADVENT
· THE NEW COVENANT ·
BY CHARLIE DANIELS

We know that Christmas celebrates the birth of Jesus Christ, our savior, and I hope this Christmas season we will all take some time to ponder the vastness of God's sacrifice and His boundless love for us, His children. The Bible refers to Jesus as "the Lamb slain from the foundation of the world" (Revelation 13:8), which tells us that God's ultimate plan of salvation was in place from the time He created the earth.

The Bible also says that "without the shedding of blood there is no forgiveness of sin" (Hebrews 9:22), and in the Mosaic Law, God instituted animal sacrifice which embodied the giving of the very best, an animal without defect or mark, in other words something dear to your heart that you didn't really want to part with. This practice meant an innocent animal's blood would be shed for the forgiveness of sin.

These sacrifices had to be carried out over and over and it all became very legalistic, a cycle of sin and sacrifice, never really reaching the point of repentance and atonement that God desired. Men who lived in strict adherence to the law took license to do anything that wasn't specifically forbidden and appropriated the homes of widows and orphans and took unfair advantage of the poor and helpless. They lived by the letter of the law but not by the spirit of the law, defiling the commandment to "Love thy neighbor as thyself" (Leviticus 19:18).

Jesus came to earth to bring a New Covenant, He said He did not come to earth to do away with the law and prophets but to fulfill them, a covenant of conscience and compassion, adhering to the commandments of God by the dictates of the heart, not the intellect. And this New Covenant required only one shedding of blood, the blood of our Creator Who loved us so much that He left the indescribable splendor of Heaven to suffer the most horrible death imaginable.

READ PSALM 80:1–7, 17–19

When Jesus died, the curtain covering the entrance to the Holy of Holies in the Temple in Jerusalem tore in half, signifying that no longer would mankind have to approach God for forgiveness and favor through a third party, a priest, but that we can enter the very presence of Almighty God in the name of His Son, and make our desires known to Him without the shedding of blood, because the blood of Jesus was shed once and for all to cover the sins of mankind (Hebrews 10:10).

Accepting the salvation of Jesus Christ is a simple act. The Bible says "If you declare with your mouth, 'Jesus is Lord,' and believe in your heart that God raised him from the dead, you will be saved" (Romans 10:9).

We enter the presence of God in humility, belief, and repentance. To repent simply means to turn away, and accept that Jesus died and shed His blood that we might receive forgiveness and salvation, and if we sin again, and we will, that when we ask we will be forgiven.

Jesus Christ, Son of God, Savior of mankind, "the way, the truth and the life," is the only path to God and eternal salvation.

The 2nd Sunday of ADVENT

· THE BIRTH ·

BY CHARLIE DANIELS

The actual birth of Jesus, although attended by choirs of angels, multitudes of heavenly hosts, and a special star that stood over the place He was born, was, in reality, a most humble affair. Earthly kings are born in palaces, but the King of the Universe was born in a stable and laid in a feed trough and surrounded by animals.

The first people to be notified about the earth-shaking event were not the religious leaders of the day, the self-righteous Pharisees, the king, or the Roman conquerors, but a band of lowly shepherds tending sheep in the Judean wilderness. I've often wondered what the shepherds thought when angels appeared and told them that the long awaited Messiah of Israel had been born in Bethlehem.

READ ISAIAH 40:1–11

The Bible says they were "sore afraid" (Luke 2:9) but the angel reassured them and gave them the good news, and this part is fascinating to say the least. The angel said, "And this shall be a sign unto you; Ye shall find the babe wrapped in swaddling clothes, lying in a manger" (Luke 2:12), so it must have been God's will that the first eyes to behold the King of Kings would be those of common men.

The Bible tells us that God is no respecter of persons; your station in life, no matter how lofty, means nothing to Him. Man looks at rank, station, and worldly grandeur and accomplishment, but Almighty God looks on the inside, at the heart, where the true measure of a man's worth is taken.

All throughout the New Testament we find Jesus in the company of the everyday working class people, while He criticized the elitist Pharisees for their hypocrisy and unbelief. He healed blind beggars and leprous outcasts. He multiplied a few pieces of bread and fish into enough to feed the thousands of every-day people who followed Him around. He chose his disciples from among fishermen, revolutionaries, and ordinary working class folk.

The first person to be saved after Jesus was nailed to the cross was a common criminal, a thief hanging on a cross next to Jesus, when, in the last agonizing hours of his life he asked Jesus to remember him when He came into His Kingdom.

In Jesus' day the Jewish faith was centered around the Temple. The Temple was controlled by a council of religious leaders called the Sanhedrin, and the decrees they passed down and the decisions they made were the final word on anything to do with Judaism.

The Sanhedrin—comprised of Pharisees and Sadducees—were experts on Mosiac Law, and their interpretation was a law unto itself. Jesus called them a brood of vipers who tied up heavy burdens and laid them on men's shoulders, while they themselves were unwilling to move them by so much as a finger. He said they did their good deeds to be noticed by men. He said for us to come to Him because His yoke is easy and His burden is light, a New Covenant, a new way, a salvation of the heart, not the intellect.

Jesus Christ, Son of God, meek and lowly, born in a stable, Almighty God, reveals to the most humble among us that His salvation is equally available to all.

The 3rd Sunday of ADVENT
· THE GIFT ·
BY CHARLIE DANIELS

I believe that the hardest thing for us to understand about the salvation of Jesus Christ is its simplicity. There is no required ritual—like praying prescribed prayers so many times per day, no pilgrimage to make, no rigid ceremonies, mode of dress, penance to pay, no self-immolation, no feats performed—just belief, repentance, and acceptance.

Believe in your heart, confess with your mouth, go forth and live according to His teachings, and know that should you slip up, His forgiveness is readily available to you. Romans 10:9 says "If you declare with your mouth, 'Jesus is Lord,' and believe in your heart that God raised him from the dead, you will be saved."

All through the ages men have tried to make the process of salvation more complex by demanding that their followers ascribe to their narrow interpretation of the scriptures combining Old Testament law with New Testament teachings, and in doing so complicate the simple process of Christ's salvation to the point that people find it impossible and wander off into the darkness.

Jesus said that He didn't come to do away with the law and prophets but to fulfill them (Matthew 5:17). Under the Old Covenant many who followed the letter of the law (including tithing from the herbs in their gardens) failed miserably in following the spirit of the law, depriving the needy and wallowing in self-righteousness.

God's gift to mankind puts His salvation within the reach of all who would humble themselves; acknowledge that Jesus Christ is the Son of God and the only path to God; realize and confess that they need a Savior, honestly regret their sins, repent, or turn away from them and follow His teachings, knowing that His forgiveness is readily available to all who in truth try to serve Him.

The Bible says that it is more blessed to give than to receive, and we are admonished time and time again to help widows and orphans and give to the poor, and the Christmas season seems to quicken the hearts of many to address the needs they see around them, and that's a good thing.

So many times, our giving at Christmas time becomes almost ritualistic, an obligation to be fulfilled, a business relationship to be courted, a quid pro quo to be maintained. But the gifts that have lasting meaning are the ones given, not for recognition or to receive something in return, nor to maintain a relationship or to curry favor, but the ones given from the heart in secret.

And the greatest gift of all is the one we shy away from most often. Answering the Great Commission, to help bring somebody to Jesus, to help them strip away the legalism and understand the love, to cut through the man-made hypocrisy and go straight to simple biblical truths, the truth that no matter what they've heard, Jesus is available to all with a sincere believing heart and a repentant spirit, and that requires us giving the greatest gift we can offer, ourselves.

READ LUKE 1:46—55

IT IS MORE *Blessed* TO GIVE THAN TO RECEIVE

Photo: Courtesy Danielle DiGregorio

The 4th Sunday of ADVENT

· SIGNS OF HIS COMING ·

BY CHARLIE DANIELS

READ LUKE 1:26–38

The birth of our Lord and Savior, which we celebrate at Christmas, was the beginning. His return will be the fulfillment. All my life I have been hearing people say that the Second Coming of Jesus Christ is near, and I'm sure it has been going on for many decades before I was born.

The Bible plainly tells us that no man can know the day or the hour, but it does not tell us that we can't know the season. Just as fruit ripens on a tree until it reaches maturity, the season of the return of the Son of Man is upon us and the actual event can't be too far behind. Hours? Days? Weeks? Decades? We have no way of knowing because it will be reckoned on God's time. But the signs of His return are all around us and rapidly falling into place.

You could say that God's prophetic time clock started on May 14, 1948, when David Ben-Gurion announced that by United Nations mandate, the State of Israel had been reborn and would be recognized as a sovereign nation. There had not been a nation of Israel since the Jewish diaspora between the sixth and eighth centuries BC when the Jews were exiled from the Land of Israel and eventually dispersed among the nations, and without a physical Israel some of the latter day prophecies could not proceed.

The signs of His coming are all around us and scream at us from the front pages of our newspapers every day. Here are some of the signs as written about in the scriptures:

SIGNS OF HIS COMING

1. Wars and rumors of wars (Matthew 24:6). Obviously taking place today.

2. The Jews returning to their land (Isaiah 11:10–12). It's been happening for well over a century as Jews from 108 nations have made the pilgrimage back to their homeland.

3. Increase of evil and wickedness (Matthew 24:12–13). Watch any newscast, pick up any newspaper—they are inundated with stories about rape, murder, gang violence, child molestation, and corruption in high places.

4. The Great Apostasy (2 Thessalonians 2:1–4). The falling away from God, old mainline churches have aligned their creed to new age acceptance of unbiblical principles, thereby ascribing to the "doctrine of demons" (1 Timothy 4:1).

5. Famines, pestilence, earthquakes (Luke 21:11). How many appeals for help to feed starving people have you seen on TV lately? A catastrophic Ebola outbreak was narrowly averted recently, bacteria are becoming increasingly antibiotic resistant, and nobody knows for sure if the next flu strain can be controlled.

6. Devastating earthquakes have rocked many parts of the world in recent years.

7. Jesus said the Gospel would be preached to all the world (Matthew 24:14), a feat that was all but impossible a few years ago, but with present day satellite technology, it's possible.

Of course this is just the tip of the prophetic iceberg, much more can be found in the Old and New Testaments. Suffice it to say this planet is rushing toward the time of Christ's return to this earth to claim His place as King of Kings and Lord of Lords.

THE BIRTH OF JESUS

Luke: **2** In those days Caesar Augustus issued a decree that a census should be taken of the entire Roman world. [2](This was the first census that took place while Quirinius was governor of Syria.) [3]And everyone went to their own town to register.

[4]So Joseph also went up from the town of Nazareth in Galilee to Judea, to Bethlehem the town of David, because he belonged to the house and line of David. [5]He went there to register with Mary, who was pledged to be married to him and was expecting a child. [6]While they were there, the time came for the baby to be born, [7]and she gave birth to her firstborn, a son. She wrapped him in cloths and placed him in a manger, because there was no guest room available for them.

[8]And there were shepherds living out in the fields nearby, keeping watch over their flocks at night. [9]An angel of the Lord appeared to them, and the glory of the Lord shone around them, and they were terrified. [10]But the angel said to them, "Do not be afraid. I bring you good news that will cause great joy for all the people. [11]Today in the town of David a Savior has been born to you; he is the Messiah, the Lord. [12]This will be a sign to you: You will find a baby wrapped in cloths and lying in a manger."

[13]Suddenly a great company of the heavenly host appeared with the angel, praising God and saying,

[14]"Glory to God in the highest heaven, and on earth peace to those on whom his favor rests."

[15]When the angels had left them and gone into heaven, the shepherds said to one another, "Let's go to Bethlehem and see this thing that has happened, which the Lord has told us about."

[16]So they hurried off and found Mary and Joseph, and the baby, who was lying in the manger. [17]When they had seen him, they spread the word concerning what had been told them about this child, [18]and all who heard it were amazed at what the shepherds said to them. [19]But Mary treasured up all these things and pondered them in her heart. [20]The shepherds returned, glorifying and praising God for all the things they had heard and seen, which were just as they had been told.

DECKING the HALLS with MUSIC

By Deborah Evans Price

I can't imagine celebrating Christmas without music, can you? Whether it's a classic Christmas carol or something new, music has a way of preparing my heart for the birth of Christ as well as setting a festive mood for this central event in human history. I'm a bit like Dustin Lynch, a self-proclaimed "Christmas nerd," who says, "I bought $80 worth of Christmas carols last year on iTunes—I'm not exaggerating. I just loaded up on them." His favorite? The Bing Crosby version of "It's Beginning to Look a Lot Like Christmas."

Not everyone grew up with an emphasis on Christmas music. If that's you, you're in good company. Vince Gill confides, "Christmas music was never a big part of my life until I met my wife Amy Grant. Now, for the last twenty years, singing Christmas music has become part of our family tradition." Among his favorites, Vince loves "Silent Night" because it's so peaceful, and "O Come All Ye Faithful" because of its beautiful melody and message.

In the case of Richard Sterban, from The Oak Ridge Boys, he's been an avid caroler from his childhood. Sterban says, "I love singing traditional Christmas carols that talk about the real true meaning of Christmas—and that's the birth of Jesus. I started caroling years ago with my youth group, the one I was a part of in church as a teenager growing up. Our youth group would go Christmas caroling at hospitals and we'd visit other shut-ins to sing traditional Christmas carols for them."

That tradition continued into his college years. Sterban recalls, "When I went to Trenton State College, we had a caroling group called The Carolers. Since you had to be a music major studying voice, you can imagine this vocal group was pretty good. We would go from dormitory to dormitory at my college and sing traditional Christmas carols. My college was not a Christian school. It's a secular liberal arts school. Still, we sang traditional religious carols that talked about the birth of Jesus. So I started that tradition at an early age and I've carried it up to this very day."

And, if you've had a chance to catch The Oak Ridge Boys on their wonderful annual Christmas tour, you'll find that, as Sterban says, "It's not about Santa Claus or the romantic side of Christmas or that sort of thing. We always end these shows singing about the true meaning of Christmas and that, of course, is the birth of Jesus. I'm glad I started singing Christmas carols at a very early age. I've been able to maintain that tradition throughout my life. I've turned seventy-two, and I'm still doing it!"

merry Christmas!

CHRISTMAS MUSIC THEN and NOW

Alan Jackson has a lot of favorite Christmas carols, but the one at the top of his playlist is the classic tune, "Up on the House Top" which dates way back to 1864. Written by Benjamin Hanby and re-recorded by numerous artists, perhaps the most famous rendition was recorded by Gene Autry. Even though Jackson admits it is kind of a "silly" song, he likes it "because my mama sang it a lot. It's one you don't hear very much, but I always think of my mama singing it all the time at Christmas."

The only "secular" Christmas song predating "Up on the House Top" is "Jingle Bells" which was originally released in 1857 and happens to be the favorite of Chris Thompson (Eli Young Band). Thompson says, "I love this song because it encapsulates the joy of Christmas. You can't help but have joy when you hear that song."

When it comes to newer Christmas music, Florida Georgia Line members Tyler Hubbard and Brian Kelley both love "Mary, Did You Know?" written by Nashville songwriters Mark Lowry and Buddy Greene. In the case of Darius Rucker, he fulfilled a life-long dream by recording Home for the Holidays, a Christmas album, in 2014. He included two originals, one titled "What God Wants for Christmas."

Rucker explains, "The song is about a guy who is in his car looking at Christmas happening all around him—people shopping, manger scenes, and all that stuff. Then all of a sudden, he thinks, 'I wonder what God wants for Christmas.'" His favorite part of the song is at the end when he sings, "I wonder what God wants for Christmas, by now we ought to know." Why is that especially meaningful? Rucker says, "Because all the great teachings that the Bible gives us are what God wants for Christmas—peace on earth, be good to each other." He adds, "One of my favorite lines is 'more sister, more brother, more loving one another.'

That's what He's taught us. That's what Jesus came and died for, namely, for us to live that way."

In the case of Jimmy Wayne, a Christmas song sung by a prisoner literally changed his life. Jimmy tells it best:

When I was in school, a prison inmate named Jody Lee Hager came to our school to talk to students about making the right choices. The prison would send him around to the schools to tell the children, "Think smart. Don't be like me." That day he sang a Christmas song he had written called, "For Days Like This." I was thinking, "Why is he singing a Christmas song in the springtime?"

But his song was so amazing that it inspired me to buy a guitar that weekend at a yard sale. It also inspired me to go to the prison and beg the warden to let me come in and sit down with Jody Lee to learn guitar from him. I visited him each week until he got out of prison. I lost contact with him because he's kind of a rambler. About three years ago, I was listening to the radio at Christmastime and I thought about the song Jody sang in my school twenty years before. I decided to look him up on the internet.

I called and said, "You may not know who this is, but you inspired me to do what I'm doing today. I was thinking about you and wanted to know how you are doing." Jody told me that he got out of prison, got a record deal, got a publishing deal in Nashville, and moved there. Sadly, he lost the deal within a month due to drugs. He explained how he went back to prison and used to lay in his prison cell listening to me singing on the radio.

Jody said, "Man, I could not believe that you were the kid that I mentored in jail—and you went off and lived my dream." I said, "So what is your dream?" He said, "My dad told me, 'Son, you need to lay brick, just learn to lay brick and work.' But Jody didn't want to become a mason. He just wanted to play at the Grand Ole Opry.

When I asked him if his dad was still alive, Jody said he was but that he was dying. I said, "In about a week and a half I have a spot on the Grand Ole Opry, a Saturday night show and they give me a chance to do two songs. Can you come to Nashville and walk out on that stage and sing 'For Days Like This,' the song that inspired me to do what I'm doing?" Whoever gets a chance to be inspired by somebody, their hero, and then have a chance to give it back to them?

On December 22, 2012, I sang a song at the Grand Ole Opry and then introduced him. Jody walked out on stage to sing his song—and got a standing ovation. The message of the song is that "Jesus was born for days like this." You see, when Jody was in prison, he had just got beat up and they threw him in the hole. He wrote this song in the hole. Jesus was born for days like this—like being in prison on Christmas.

The chorus lyrics are:
He was born for days like this
And for the ones who are and aren't missed
When this world forgets that you even exist
He was born for days like this

HOME *for* a WHITE CHRISTMAS

For most, Christmas is a time when families gather together to celebrate, sing, and make memories—which is why "I'll Be Home for Christmas" resonates with so many country artists. Marty Roe from Diamond Rio says, "That one always rings true to me being a touring musician living my life on the road." Neal McCoy loves that song "because we are gone so much" even though he did miss Christmas once because he was performing for the troops on a USO Tour in Afghanistan. Likewise, Mike Eli (Eli Young Band) says, "There have been so many years that we've been on the road so much that getting home for the holidays to spend some good Christmas time with your family, to go see the parents, your sisters, and the nephews and nieces—it's such a great feeling."

Interestingly, Lee Greenwood was named after Melvin Torme, who originally wrote "I'll Be Home for Christmas." Lee explains, "My mother named me 'Melvin Lee Greenwood' when I was born. I changed my name to 'Lee Melvin Greenwood' because I didn't like the two syllables at the beginning. You see, I grew up on a farm and at dinner time they would go 'Meeelviiin.' I hated that so I changed my first name to "Lee" so they couldn't do that with one syllable. 'I'll Be Home for Christmas' was one of my mother's favorite songs. She used to play it on the piano for us at Christmas time, so that's my favorite, too."

Being home to celebrate Christmas may be at the top of their wish list, but having a "White Christmas" is a close second. Howard Bellamy always enjoys singing this tune during the annual Bellamy Brothers Tropical Christmas show, while it resonates with Billy Currington "because I was always dreaming of a White Christmas. Where I lived in South Georgia, we don't get a white Christmas." For Phil Vassar there's nothing better than the "old school guys singing this stuff. I don't know what it is but with Bing Crosby singing 'White Christmas' there's just something magical about it."

Of course, you don't have to have the voice of Nat King Cole or Frank Sinatra to enjoy a special time singing together as a family. To help you and yours set the stage for a Christmas filled with music in the home, here's a deeper dive into five Country Faith Christmas favorites.

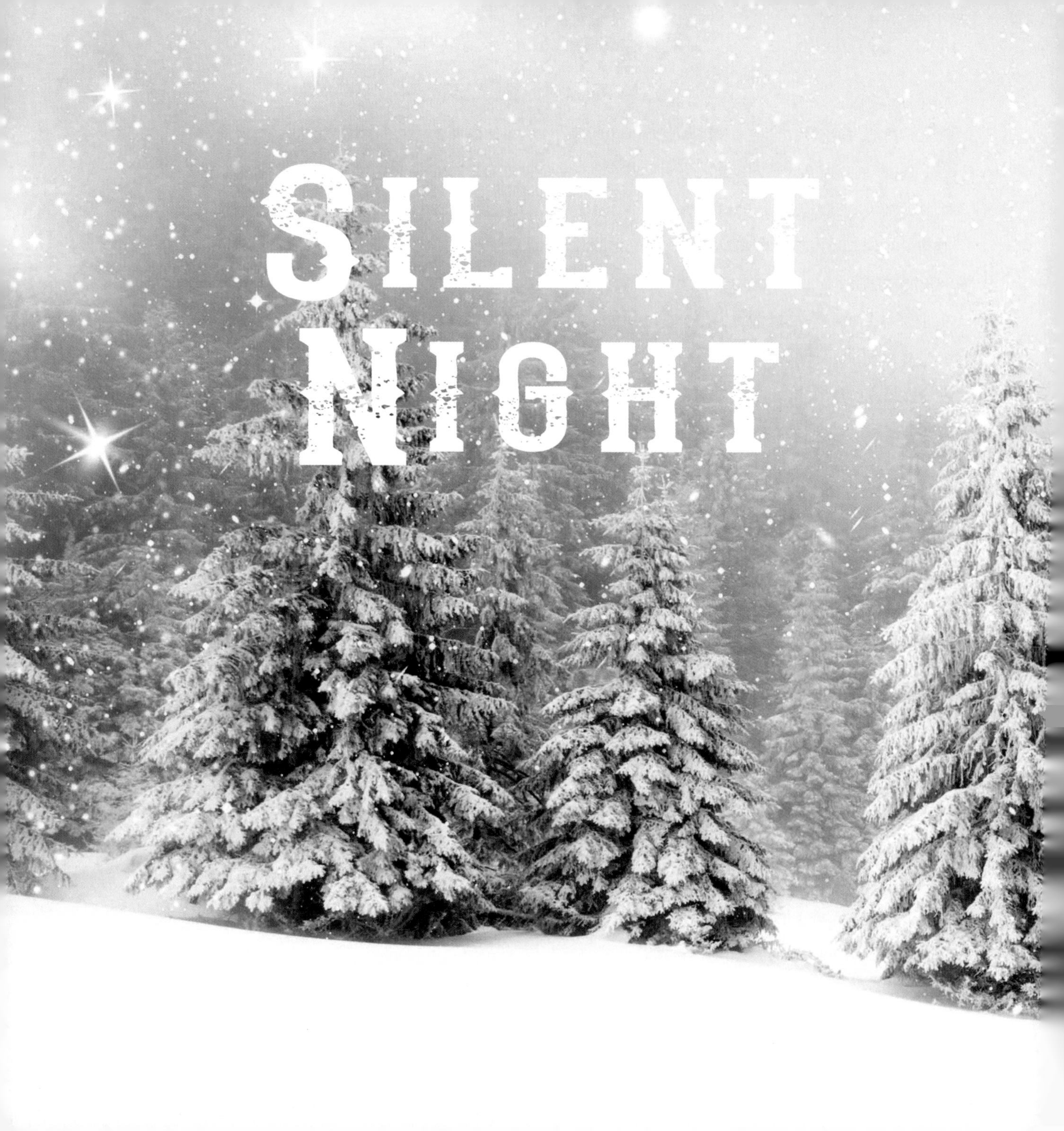
SILENT
NIGHT

Of the Christmas carols that I really love, "Silent Night" is in my top five. I'm a lot like Eric Paslay, who says, "I'm a sucker for the slow ones that everyone can sing harmony to—and 'Silent Night' says the real meaning of Christmas." Mickey Guyton says, "The melody always gives me chills" while Gene Johnson of Diamond Rio says this song moves him deeply because "it's about the true Christmas and the birth of Christ. It's just one of those songs that almost brings me to tears when we'd sing it. It's one of the first carols that I can remember from childhood. Of all the songs, that's the one I just really took to—and it's still my favorite."

Charlie Daniels put it this way: "'Silent Night' epitomizes Christmas to me. It's been a part of Christmas as long as I can remember wherever I happened to be, whatever I happened to be doing. No matter what else was playing, or whatever else was popular at the time, it's always 'Silent Night.' It's just hard to imagine Christmas time without it."

Fans young and old agree with Daniels because "Silent Night" is the most popular carol ever recorded—with more than seven hundred copyrighted renditions! Lee Brice is also a big fan of this carol. He says, "'Silent Night' was always my thing. There's so much truth in it and it takes me back to that night when Jesus was born." Which is part of the reason Brenda Lee says, "I do that song in my Christmas show and I cry every time I sing it—it's just gorgeous."

Colton Swon put it this way: "You definitely have the reason for the season in there with 'Silent Night.' It's basically talking about the whole reason that we celebrate Christmas. Without Christ and the birth of Christ, we are nothing. It would just be a bunch of greedy people giving each other presents. This carol kind of sums it all up because it's the reason we are all here." Indeed, if Jesus hadn't been born on that silent night more than two thousand years ago, we wouldn't be celebrating the Ultimate Gift to mankind—a Savior whose birth changes everything!

Silent night, Holy night
All is calm, all is bright
Round yon virgin, mother and child
Holy infant, so tender and mild
Sleep in heavenly peace,
Sleep in heavenly peace.

Silent night, Holy night
Son of God, love's pure light
Radiant beams from thy holy face
With the dawn of redeeming grace,
Jesus, Lord at thy birth
Jesus, Lord at thy birth.

Silent night, Holy night
Shepherds quake, at the sight
Glories stream from heaven above
Heavenly hosts sing Hallelujah.
Christ the Savior is born,
Christ the Savior is born.

The precise origin of this carol is a bit tricky to pin down. Some suggest that the words and the music were written separately from each other—with the lyrics emerging from a Latin text in Germany during the early 1700s while the music dates back to France in the fifteenth century. To be sure, this Christian hymn has been a favorite for Advent because the lyrics highlight several names of Jesus found in Scripture ("Rod of Jesse" from Isaiah 11:1, "Day-Spring" from Luke 1:78, "Key of David" from Isaiah 22:22) coupled with an emotionally evocative, if not downright haunting, melody.

Diamond Rio's Dana Williams is a big fan of the older songs and laments that "Christmas music has just gotten to where you don't do as many of the classic Christmas carols anymore. But 'O Come, O Come Emanuel' just knocks me out. That song is all about the birth of Christ." I'm with Dana—it still knocks me out after all of these years, too!

O come, O come, Emmanuel
And ransom captive Israel
That mourns in lonely exile here
Until the Son of God appear.
Rejoice! Rejoice! Emmanuel
Shall come to thee, O Israel.

O come, Thou Rod of Jesse, free
Thine own from Satan's tyranny
From depths of Hell Thy people save
And give them victory o'er the grave.
Rejoice! Rejoice! Emmanuel
Shall come to thee, O Israel.

O come, Thou Day-Spring, come and cheer
Our spirits by Thine advent here
Disperse the gloomy clouds of night
And death's dark shadows put to flight.
Rejoice! Rejoice! Emmanuel
Shall come to thee, O Israel.

O come, Thou Key of David, come,
And open wide our heavenly home;
Make safe the way that leads on high,
And close the path to misery.
Rejoice! Rejoice! Emmanuel
Shall come to thee, O Israel.

O come, O come, Thou Lord of might,
Who to Thy tribes, on Sinai's height,
In ancient times did'st give the Law,
In cloud, and majesty and awe.
Rejoice! Rejoice! Emmanuel
Shall come to thee, O Israel.

Topping the Christmas carol list for Canaan Smith is "O Holy Night." He likes the fact that "it's not jingly and happy sounding. It's really kind of eerie. It's almost haunting. We would always go to candle light service on Christmas Eve. Maybe that's why it's one of my favorite songs because I was used to candles being lit as we gathered in a room to celebrate the most holy moment of all time. That song just sets up the moment."

The Roys recorded their first Christmas album in 2014. "O Holy Night" was at the top of the list of songs they wanted to record because, as Lee Roy says, "it encompasses everything that is Christmas since Christmas is about the birth of our Savior Jesus." Elaine Roy agrees, adding, "When I hear that song it always stops me in my tracks and makes me pause for a moment and really listen."

"O Holy Night" is also Wade Hayes's favorite carol because he says, "that song is exactly what it's all about. It's talking about Christ's birth and the chords are so perfect with a beautiful melody." Wade especially likes John Berry or Glen Campbell's version of it. For Reba McEntire, it's her favorite Christmas song because "it is so spiritual to me and I love the harmonies. The melody is so beautiful—I love minor keys—and it's got a wonderful chord progression."

O Holy Night
The stars are brightly shining
It is the night of our dear Savior's birth
Long lay the world in sin and error pining
'Til He appeared and the soul felt its worth
A thrill of hope the weary world rejoices
For yonder breaks a new and glorious morn.
Fall on your knees, O hear the angels' voices.
O night divine, O night when Christ was born,
O night divine, O night, O night divine.

Led by the light of Faith serenely beaming,
With glowing hearts by His cradle we stand.
So led by light of a star sweetly gleaming,
Here came the wise men from Orient land.
The King of Kings lay thus in lowly manger;
In all our trials born to be our friend.
He knows our need, to our weakness is no stranger,
Behold your King! Before Him lowly bend!
Behold your King! Before Him lowly bend!

Truly He taught us to love one another;
His law is love and His gospel is peace.
Chains shall He break for the slave is our brother;
And in His name all oppression shall cease.
Sweet hymns of joy in grateful chorus raise we,
Let all within us praise His holy name.
Christ is the Lord! O praise His Name forever,
His power and glory evermore proclaim.
O night divine, O night, O night divine.

Dating back to the early 1900s, "Go Tell It on the Mountain" is an African American spiritual perennial favorite. It's been rerecorded by dozens of gospel, pop, and country artists including The Kingston Trio, Mahalia Jackson, The Blind Boys of Alabama, Frank Sinatra with Bing Crosby, Dolly Parton, Anne Murray, Little Big Town, and Sara Evans. Hunter Hayes recorded his version of this classic carol because "I'm attached to it. I've always loved it."

Hayes recalls growing up listening to a Garth Brooks version that he loved because "It was all bluesy and cool. But then the version I recorded was more around the time that I was studying James Taylor and his music. I studied his version and did a combination of that and another version I had heard." For Hayes it's all about the melody. He says, "I love melodies that take stories to a new level. And certain melodies just move you. I feel like it was written without much thought getting in the way. It was more about the spirit of the song that really lifts you. It also has a peacefulness and a beautiful anticipation about it that I love."

This Christmas, why not let this classic carol move you, too?

Go tell it on the mountain
Over the hills and everywhere
Go tell it on the mountain
That Jesus Christ is born

The shepherds all were watching
Over their sheep at night
When a guiding star shone from heaven
And they followed that holy light

Go tell it on the mountain
Over the hills and everywhere
Go tell it on the mountain
That Jesus Christ is born

They found a lovely manger
Where the humble Christ was born
And God sent out salvation
On that blessed Christmas morn

Go tell it on the mountain
Over the hills and everywhere
Go tell it on the mountain
That Jesus Christ is born

He brought with Him forgiveness
He lived to show us the way
He came to redeem all creation
And to wash all our sins away

Go tell it on the mountain
Over the hills and everywhere
Go tell it on the mountain
That Jesus Christ is born

If you're like me, you've probably had a song stuck in your head. You know, a catchy chorus that just won't quit. Which is why when a songwriter writes a song, he or she knows the power and importance of writing a great "hook"—that melodic line, usually in the chorus, which stays with you long after you've stopped listening to the tune. For Little Big Town's Kimberly Schlapman, this Christmas carol got her hooked from a very young age. She says, "I love that chorus, 'O come let us adore Him, O come let us adore Him.' That chorus makes me so incredibly emotional. I can remember singing that in a tiny, tiny children's choir in church."

Why has that chorus hooked her? She explains, "To me, that song is Christmas because I believe that Christmas is completely about the Savior. Sometimes I find myself during the year singing that chorus because it not only applies to the birth of Jesus, but to my everyday life because I try to make Him first and sometimes when I get caught up in my to-do lists and my expectations of myself I think, truly I need to live my life for Jesus so let me remind myself, 'O come let us adore Him' and that way I don't get so caught up in me."

Not only is this her favorite carol, but it tops the charts for Marty Raybon, Vince Gill, and David Bellamy. Jamie O'Neal—who loves caroling door-to-door—says "this carol reminds me of the togetherness Christmas brings and the peaceful feeling of celebrating Jesus's birth."

O come all ye faithful
Joyful and triumphant,
O come ye, O come ye to Bethlehem.
Come and behold Him,
Born the King of Angels;
O come, let us adore Him,
O come, let us adore Him,
O come, let us adore Him,
Christ the Lord.

O Sing, choirs of angels,
Sing in exultation,
Sing all that hear in heaven God's holy word.
Give to our Father glory in the Highest;
O come, let us adore Him,
O come, let us adore Him,
O come, let us adore Him,
Christ the Lord.

All Hail! Lord, we greet Thee,
Born this happy morning,
O Jesus! for evermore be Thy name adored.
Word of the Father, now in flesh appearing;
O come, let us adore Him,
O come, let us adore Him,
O come, let us adore Him,
Christ the Lord

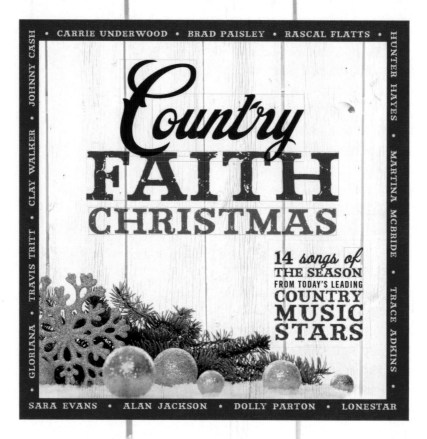

Country FAITH CHRISTMAS

CARRIE UNDERWOOD • BRAD PAISLEY • RASCAL FLATTS

JOHNNY CASH • CLAY WALKER • TRAVIS TRITT • GLORIANA

HUNTER HAYES • MARTINA McBRIDE • TRACE ADKINS

14 *songs of* THE SEASON FROM TODAY'S LEADING COUNTRY MUSIC STARS

SARA EVANS • ALAN JACKSON • DOLLY PARTON • LONESTAR

Country *Faith Christmas* is the perfect companion collection of favorite holiday songs sung by your favorite Country artists! 14 of Country music's biggest artists come together to share personal songs of Christmas in this all-star collection. Featuring songs from today's most popular artists like Carrie Underwood, Brad Paisley, Hunter Hayes and Rascal Flatts, to cherished heritage artists like Alan Jackson, Dolly Parton, and Johnny Cash, this compilation is perfect for Country fans young and old alike!

ALSO AVAILABLE:
Country Faith. 15 of Country music's biggest artists share personal songs of faith in this inspirational collection!

Look for Country Faith products online and at your favorite retailer.   www.countryfaith.com

REGNERY FAITH   word   CURB RECORDS   curb.com